The high cost of following Christ is a major theme in the Gospels. A fickle or indifferent disciple is a contradiction. And Christ's own summons to discipleship is impossible to harmonize with the laid-back, seeker-sensitive, superficial religion practiced by so many people today who claim to be followers of Christ. Believers constantly need to be reminded of these truths. Dr. Lawson's exposition of Luke 14:25-35 distills the vital message and presents it in a robust and penetrating way. Here is a book every Christian ought to read and seriously take to heart.

JOHN MACARTHUR,
President, The Master's University and Seminary and
Pastor-Teacher, Grace Community Church, Sun Valley, California

With compassion, patience, and clarity, Dr. Lawson sets before the reader a clear exposition of the gospel and the gospel call according to Jesus. He writes as he preaches - with a tenacious grip on the Scriptures and a pastor's heart that longs for the salvation of the lost and the edification of the church. This book is a "must read" for all! The unconverted will hear the gospel; the Christian will find the true road to devotion and joy; the minister will be instructed in the task of biblical gospel preaching, ensuring salvation both for himself and for those who hear him (1 Tim. 4:16).

PAUL WASHER,
President, Heart Cry Ministry,
Radford, Virginia

Like a master builder Steve Lawson gives us the foundation of Jesus' own words to erect a frame showing the cost, demands, gains and losses of following Christ. In doing so, Dr. Lawson gives us a strong and firm edifice that brings glory to Him and His truth.

R. C. SPROUL,
Founder and Chairman of Ligonier Ministries,
Chancellor of Reformation Bible College, Sanford, Florida

Steven J. Lawson

WHOEVER DOES NOT

The CARRY HIS

OWN CROSS Cost

AND COME AFTER ME

*What it takes
to follow Jesus* CANNOT

BE MY DISCIPLE

**CHRISTIAN
FOCUS**

paperback ISBN 978-1-78191-955-2
mobi ISBN 978-1-78191-957-6
epub ISBN 978-1-78191-956-9

10 9 8 7 6 5 4 3 2 1

Published in 2017
by
Christian Focus Publications Ltd,
Geanies House, Fearn, Tain, Ross-shire,
Scotland IV20 1TW, UK.

www.christianfocus.com

Cover design by Paul Lewis

Printed by Bell & Bain, Glasgow

CONTENTS

DEDICATED TO

AUSTIN T. DUNCAN,
A FAITHFUL FRIEND IN MINISTRY

who has been an invaluable asset
and constant encourager to me.

PREFACE

This is a book I had to write. Why do I say that? Because I want those who have not yet come to know Jesus Christ to commit their lives to Him and become His followers. The greatest joy in life is to know Jesus personally. Only a life committed to Him will find ultimate fulfillment. If you are not there yet, my desire is that you enter into a personal relationship with Him today. I want to help you make that life-changing commitment.

However, I have another concern – that large numbers of people, who either attend church or who are morally good people, wrongly presume that they have a right relationship with God. Tragically, though, they have never actually committed their lives to Him. Surely, they know *about* Jesus. They have a degree of knowledge about Him in their heads, but they do not truly know Him in their hearts. They have been lulled into a false sense of assurance about salvation that they do not possess. Churches are full of such people. If this is you, I want to help you see that you have not yet come to the saving knowledge of Jesus Christ. In turn, I want to help point you to Him.

In order for this to happen, you need to hear what is required to be a genuine follower of Christ. In many pulpits, the message of salvation has been obscured, if not altered. As a result, many people pull up short of what it truly is to be an authentic believer in Jesus. I fear that many think they are trusting in Him, but, in reality, have not yet done so. Instead, they have believed in a sugar-coated message with a shallow imitation of the real truth. The result is a synthetic salvation.

We need to hear the gospel preached from the greatest Preacher of all, Jesus Christ Himself. We need to be taught by the very One whose gospel it is. What Jesus had to say about following Him has been largely diluted. I believe that He does not even recognize most of what is presented as the gospel today. We desperately need to hear the unvarnished truth on this ultimate issue. No one can follow Jesus until they first hear the truth.

In His earthly ministry, there was not one canned approach that Jesus used in presenting the gospel to people. To Nicodemus, a ruler of the Jews, He used the analogy of the new birth. To the Samaritan woman, He used the metaphor of drinking living water. To another crowd, He used the picture of an ox submitting to a yoke. Many other examples could be given of the different ways that Jesus chose to represent the gospel message. He was careful to adapt each presentation of the truth to each individual person in each unique setting. The gospel message was always the same, but the way it was presented varied with each situation.

That said, there was one gospel presentation used by Jesus that needs to be heard again today. I refer to what He spoke to a large crowd as recorded in Luke 14:25-35. In this passage, there are several images used by Jesus that are presently too often neglected. These requirements include the necessity of self-denial, cross-bearing, counting the cost, surrendering to Christ, and authentic discipleship. Such necessary truths in the gospel sound foreign to many ears today. However, they cannot be ignored and must be acted upon.

In this message, Jesus did not give a watered-down version of the truth. He required the kind of genuine commitment by which one gains entrance into the kingdom of God. I want to help you see what is required in beginning an authentic relationship with Christ. These words spoken by the Lord will be a critical factor in reevaluating whether or not you have genuinely believed in Him.

For you who have not yet come to faith in Jesus Christ, my desire is that what He said so long ago will be used to bring you to Himself. For those of you who have already believed in Him, I trust that His message will challenge you to a deeper walk with Him.

I want the Lord Jesus to speak for Himself. May He use this book with its careful look at Luke 14:25-35 to help you grasp what it is to follow Him. In this discovery, may He guide you into a personal relationship with Him.

Blessings in Christ,

Steven J. Lawson
Dallas, Texas

1

COME FOLLOW

'Come after Me' (Luke 14:27).

To follow Jesus Christ is the greatest adventure in all of life. It involves the pursuit of life's greatest purpose – the glory that belongs to Christ alone. It meets life's greatest need – the forgiveness of sin that only Jesus can give. It gives life's greatest pleasure – the joy that comes exclusively from knowing Christ. It involves the greatest partnership in life – the fellowship of walking closely with Jesus. It imparts the greatest teaching in life – the wisdom that Christ alone possesses. It infuses the greatest power in life – the grace of Jesus Christ to live triumphantly. It leads to the greatest destination after life – the immediate presence of Jesus Himself in heaven.

There is no journey that can compare with this one. It will take you from where you are to where you need to be. It will take you through all of life's many experiences, including your greatest moments and darkest nights. This journey with Christ will enable you to live as God intends you to live. As you follow in His footsteps, you will find the real purpose for which you were made. Moreover, it will ultimately lead you home to heaven, to the very throne of God. No pursuit in life even begins to compare to this journey of following Jesus.

A Spiritual Journey

When Jesus calls us to come after Him, He is comparing Christianity to a path that His followers are to walk down. He personally invites us to embark on this spiritual journey. By this summons, He is not calling us to a physical walk with Him. He is not urging us to put one foot in front of the other and, literally, come after Him. What He is requiring is far deeper than for us to travel a mere dusty road with Him. He is instead speaking in spiritual terms. He is inviting us to follow Him in our hearts. He calls us to take steps of faith and follow His direction for our lives.

This spiritual journey refers to how we live our daily lives. It concerns the course that we take in life. Jesus is referring to the path we pursue and the steps we take in this world. Involved in this journey are our thoughts, actions, and even our motives and desires. Jesus is addressing what is taking place inside of our soul that drives and directs us.

When The Master Calls

Our focus in these pages will be upon one particular encounter that Jesus had with a large crowd that was going along with Him. For the most part, they gave every impression of being His disciples. They were walking with Him and were attentive to His words. They had closest proximity to Him. But the reality was that most of them were only curious about Jesus and largely uncommitted – and unconverted.

Following Jesus had become the popular thing to do, and He knew it. With a genuine concern for them, Christ stopped and turned around to address them. What He spoke were strong words that made it not easier, but actually harder, to follow Him. Jesus called for the full-scale commitment of their lives to Him when He said:

'If anyone comes to Me, and does not hate his own father and mother and wife and children and brothers and sisters, yes, and even his own life, he cannot be My disciple. Whoever does not carry his own cross and come after Me cannot be My disciple. For which one of you, when he wants to build a tower, does not first sit down and calculate the cost to see if he has enough to complete it? Otherwise, when he has laid a foundation and is not able to finish, all who observe it begin to ridicule him, saying, "This man began to build and was not able to finish." Or what king, when he sets out to meet another king in battle, will not first sit down and consider whether he is strong enough with ten thousand *men* to encounter the one coming against him with twenty thousand? Or else, while the other is still far away, he sends a delegation and asks for terms of peace. So then, none of you can be My disciple who does not give up all his own possessions. 'Therefore, salt is good; but if even salt has become tasteless, with what will it be seasoned? It is useless either for the soil or for the manure pile; it is thrown out. He who has ears to hear, let him hear' (Luke 14:26-35).

Not Sugarcoated

These provocative words were spoken toward the end of Jesus' three-year ministry, during His final journey to Jerusalem. In mere months, He will be crucified upon a Roman cross in this very city, the headquarters for the religious establishment in Israel. Jesus had little time remaining on this earth. This was not a moment to mince words. Neither was it a time to sugarcoat the message or smooth-talk the crowd. The issues were too great, and the time was too short.

In this critical instance, Jesus spoke words that were direct and demanding, even difficult for them to hear. These words were necessary and appropriate to the moment. The forceful tone was in keeping with the weightiness of the subject matter. The impact of these words was intended to awaken the spiritually dead among them. Jesus had to speak as He did in order to capture the attention of those who were lethargic. He called them to follow Him in a new journey through life that would one day lead them to the throne of God. What Jesus said to them, He says to us.

Where The Journey Begins

This journey begins the moment we come to faith in Jesus Christ. Becoming a follower of Jesus starts when we commit our lives to Him. This relationship does not commence when we simply join a religious crowd or try to become a good person. Instead, it starts when we come to the place of entrusting our life to Him. This requires the full commitment of all that we are to Jesus Christ.

To begin this journey costs us nothing. There is no amount of good works we could ever perform that could earn us a place on this path with Jesus. There is no toll for us to pay to enter onto this way. There is no moral standard for us to meet. There is no spiritual ladder for us to climb. There are no rituals for us to perform. There are no ceremonies for us to attend. There is absolutely nothing we can do to merit starting this journey with Christ.

We enter into this spiritual relationship with Him by faith. The Bible says: 'For by grace you have been saved through faith; and that not of yourselves, *it is* the gift of God; not as a result of works, so that no one may boast'(Eph. 2:8-9). Simply put, securing a starting position on this journey cannot be earned by our works. Instead, it is entered into by faith alone in Him.

How the Journey Continues

This commitment to Jesus Christ is the beginning of a whole new walk. Previously, we had been walking according to the course of this world. We had been going in the direction of the world. It was a life pursuit in which we did what we wanted, how we wanted, when we wanted, with whom we wanted. We were traveling on a broad path that tolerated any manner of life. But when we come to Christ by faith, this new journey begins to take us in an entirely new direction.

Following Jesus means we no longer go our own way. We no longer follow the flow of the crowd. We begin to walk a new path that is headed in a new direction. We walk as Jesus walked and imitate Him. We start to obey the word of God as Jesus did while He was here on the earth. We are to love people as He loved, even those who are most difficult to love. We are to act as He acted and react as He reacted in each situation. We are to meet the many challenges in life as He did, with supreme confidence in God.

What the Journey Provides

Following Jesus on this journey provides us with the greatest blessings we could ever receive. When we commit our life to Him, we receive the immediate forgiveness of our sins through the death of Christ. The penalties for our transgressions are removed from our record in heaven. All charges brought against us are cancelled. We are clothed with the perfect righteousness of Christ. This gives us full acceptance with holy God in heaven. By the death of Jesus, we are set free from our bondage to sin. Christ comes to live in us, never to leave us.

Coming after Christ directly leads us into the will of God for our lives. The path that God has chosen for us leads to the abundant life that only Jesus can give. Following Jesus provides us with the fullness of God's blessings. When we walk with Him, He promises that we are 'blessed' with deep contentment and true happiness (Matt. 5:3-12). Jesus gives to those who believe in Him the Holy Spirit, who gives us the strength to walk through this world (John 14:16-17). The Spirit is another Helper who will advise and guide us on the chosen path. The Spirit will comfort us when we are discouraged, exhort us when we are complacent, and convict us when we stray.

Jesus further gives us His peace that is unlike anything this world can give (John 14:27). This peace is the calming tranquility of heart in the midst of our many difficulties. Jesus likewise gives joy to those of us who follow Him (John 15:11). He enables us to live triumphantly in the face of our challenges. He gives us His fellowship as we walk with Him daily. He provides us with His direction through the confusing maze of this world. He provides for all our needs according to His riches in glory and causes everything to work together for our good.

What the Journey Costs

Following Jesus is a journey that comes at a high price. This is not a relationship to be entered into lightly. This decision requires the commitment of our entire life to Jesus Christ. Coming to Christ takes priority over every other pursuit in life. It necessitates the submission of our wills to Him as we surrender to His lordship. This path requires our sacrifice and, at times, even our suffering for Him. To be sure, Jesus will not follow us, we are called to follow Him.

Following Christ will cost us much. It will cost us our old way of life and forfeiting our past sins. It will cost us a life of ease and living for this world. It will cost us old habits and even old associations. It will cost us following our own agenda for how we think our life should work. It will cost us our time and treasure to spread the gospel message. It will cost us suffering for being identified with Him. It will cost us varying degrees of opposition and persecution from the world. It may even cost us our life. But in the end, we gain far more than we lose.

Where the Journey Leads

Finally, this journey leads to heaven where He Himself is seated at the right hand of God the Father. Following Jesus in this life ushers us into His immediate presence in the world to come. It leads us to the place above where He is being worshiped by all believers, down through the centuries, who have put their faith in Him. This journey will lead us to where an untold number of angels are praising Him.

No journey that has ever been undertaken leads to such a glorious destination. Following Jesus leads us upward to a far better place than this world. It ushers us to the heights of heaven and the throne of God.

Where Are You?

Before we proceed any further, let me ask you: Where are *you* in this spiritual journey with Jesus Christ? Are you a genuine follower of Jesus? Have you begun this walk with Him? Have you entrusted your life to Him? Or are you merely curious? I pray you will take this decisive step to commit your life to Christ.

If you are not already a follower of Jesus, the message that He delivered is given especially for you. Contained in this address is how to start this journey of faith with Him.

Here is how to take the first step in walking with Him. These words by Jesus reveal the entry point into a personal relationship with Him.

I want to assure you that what Jesus said so long ago will be the most important message you will ever hear. This truth will require something from you. These words spoken by Jesus are not intended to be merely interesting. They are meant to arrest your life and capture your very soul. They are intended to lead you to become a true follower of Christ.

What Jesus says in these words will also challenge the faith of every authentic disciple. This message should deepen our resolve to follow Christ. Every believer should reaffirm the foundational commitment we first made to Him. Here are necessary elements for true spirituality and growth in Christlikeness.

This is For You

No matter where you are in life, these words issued by Jesus are intended for you. Let us now carefully examine what Jesus said two thousand years ago. His words are just as relevant today as when He first spoke them centuries ago. It is worth our undivided attention to analyze and apply every statement Jesus made to this crowd. Here are life-giving words from the One who is the way, the truth, and the life, Jesus Christ our Lord.

MIXED MULTITUDES

Now large crowds were going along
with Him (Luke 14:25).

Large crowds can be an easy place to hide from commitment. The larger the crowd, the easier it is to remain anonymous. The more people that gather together, the easier it is to blend in with the masses. The bigger the assemblage, the easier it is to be undetected. This was clearly the case with the large crowds that were following Jesus Christ.

As Jesus was journeying toward Jerusalem, He was headed to the very city where He would soon be crucified. On this final trip to the holy city, massive crowds were following Him. The biblical text reads that 'large crowds' were going along with Him. This group was more than a mere gathering of people. This was an enormous convergence of humanity. The author Luke records that 'large crowds' in the plural were walking with Him. Many large crowds were merged together to form one large mass of people. The sum total of all these large crowds, collectively, comprised a vast sea of men, women, and children.

The Final Journey

For Jesus, the inevitable reality of death upon a Roman cross lay directly ahead of Him. The excruciating pain of Calvary was only months away. This would be His final journey to the holy city. Here was His last trip to the nerve center of the religious establishment of the day. As Jesus would address this crowd, this was no time to pull up short with His message. He has only this passing opportunity to address these particular people. As He does, He also speaks to each one of us.

This tremendous throng going along with Jesus was a diverse group. They were all merged together to form this one enormous multitude. The swelling numbers formed a huge horde that was walking behind Him. The excitement of the crowd was escalating as Jesus had become the most popular figure of the day. Everyone wanted to see Him with their own eyes. And everyone wanted to hear His teaching in person.

A Diverse Crowd

In this diverse group were all kinds of people who were at different places in life. Some of His followers were genuinely committed to Him. They had left behind their old ways of life and had surrendered to Him. They had entered into a new life and were following Him with their whole hearts. These were true followers of Jesus who believed He was the Son of God come to rescue ruined humanity.

Other people in the crowd were merely curious. They had never seen or heard anyone like Jesus. They were drawn to Him because He was so unlike the other religious leaders of Israel. He did not quote the other rabbis, but spoke with direct authority from God Himself. They referred to Him as Rabbi and recognized Him as a teacher come from God. They hung upon His every word, though they had not yet committed themselves to Him.

Still others were confused about who He was. Is this not the carpenter's son? Is not His mother called Mary? Could any good thing come from Nazareth? Does He have an unclean spirit? This could not be the long-awaited Messiah, could He? Was He something more? In their confusion, they were also still uncommitted.

Yet others in this large multitude were intensely religious, but were entrapped in the false system of the Pharisees. They had the outward form of religion, but not the inward reality of the living God. They were unconverted – religious, but lost. What is worse, they did not know that they were without God in their lives.

I want us to look at these groups more carefully. As we do, we will probably see ourselves in one of these categories.

The Committed Few

The first group in this large crowd were the *committed* disciples. They are the ones who were genuinely committed to Jesus. At least eleven of the twelve disciples were true believers in Him. The Lord had called them to leave behind their old lives and follow Him in this new walk of faith. He had summoned them to leave behind their past pursuits of living for themselves in order to supremely live for Him. Eleven of these men had answered that compelling call. They took the radical step of faith to follow Him.

Jesus first had invited two fishermen – John and Andrew – to stay with Him one night (John 1:35-39). They responded by giving their lives to Him. Andrew then brought his brother Simon to Jesus, who was also converted (John 1:40-42). Jesus then called Philip, saying 'Follow Me' (John 1:43). He answered the call. Philip found Nathaniel (John 1:45), who became a genuine disciple.

Jesus called a tax collector named Matthew to follow Him (Matt. 9:9). This despised publican had been living to accumulate the possessions of this world. But in that moment, he made the life-altering decision to turn his back on his old priorities. Each man instantly surrendered his life to Christ. There would be no turning back.

The Radical Choice

The rest of the disciples – including Thomas, Bartholomew, Thaddeus, James the lesser, and Simon (Mark 3:18) – made the radical choice to submit their lives to the lordship of Jesus Christ. They left behind all for which they had previously lived. Like a traveler approaching a major fork in the road, they abandoned the broad path and entered through the narrow gate that leads to life. They forsook the many to join the few. In that decisive moment, they stepped out with child-like faith to follow Him.

Is this where you are? Maybe you have forsaken your old way of living for yourself. Maybe you have received the new life that Jesus offers. Perhaps you have decided to follow Christ. If so, you are on the right path. You have much for which to be thankful.

The Curious Majority

The second group in this larger crowd would have been those who were merely curious about this popular religious figure named Jesus. They were undoubtedly attracted to Him by the remarkable things they had heard others say about Him. They had heard the reports about how He had performed miracles. Some had seen Him perform miracles. Others had heard the reports that God was with Him. He spoke as no man had ever spoken before. They had heard that He claimed to be the Son of God. Their curiosity was piqued and they had to check it out for themselves.

Many such people were drawn to follow Jesus. They wanted to see if these claims were true. Countless people had to see it for themselves. Were the reports valid that they had heard? Could this be the long-awaited Messiah? Is Jesus really the Son of God as He claims to be? This would have comprised a large segment of the following around Jesus.

The Same Today

There are countless people today who are drawn to Christ out of curiosity much like this. They are interested because Jesus remains the central figure of human history. Large masses still want to know what He says about the issues of the day. They see the good that is being done in His name. They are impressed with the Christian hospitals that are built in His name. They see the Christian ministries serving the needs of humanity. They enjoy the Christian holidays like Christmas and Easter. Many people remain similarly interested in Jesus to this day.

However, these inquisitive individuals have not committed their lives to Him. They are merely interested in the mystique about Jesus. They are drawn to the uniqueness of Jesus. They are simply a part of the larger crowd going along with Him, but they have not personally surrendered their lives to Him.

I wonder if this could describe you? Maybe you also are interested to learn more about Jesus Christ. You realize there has to be something more to life than what you have experienced so far. Maybe you sense the emptiness of this world and feel the void of being merely religious. Maybe you are giving thought to standing before God after death. Maybe you want to know what will happen when you face God. If this describes you, then you should give careful consideration to what Jesus has to say. He alone has the source of truth that will lead you into the eternal life that only He can give.

The Confused Masses
There was also a third group in the crowd following Jesus. They were those who were confused about who He was. They could not figure out His claims to be divine. Was He not a man like them? Neither could they figure out why He came into the world. They presumed He was merely a prophet sent from God. They thought He was a wise sage with profound insights into the complexities of life. They

saw Him as a good man, whose life should be emulated, but nothing beyond this.

Within this part of the large crowd, were those who were confused about the way of salvation. They presumed that the interpretation of the Pharisees was right. Surely, good people work their way to heaven. These religious leaders had convinced them that they must keep the divine law in order to gain favor with God. They misjudged the level of perfection one would need to have to keep the moral code in the Scripture. They could not grasp this was the divine standard that they could not keep, and yet they continued to try.

Faulty Perceptions

Many people are exactly like this today. They presume that they must do a prescribed amount of good works to gain acceptance into heaven. Tragically though, nothing could be further from the truth. They do not understand that all have fallen short of the glory of God (Rom. 3:23) and instead wrongly cling to the hope that God grades on the curve.

Could this faulty perception about the way of salvation describe you? Maybe you are unclear about what is required for salvation. Perhaps you are uncertain about whom to listen to in regards to obtaining the forgiveness of sin. Maybe you are perplexed about the hard sayings of Jesus concerning entrance into His kingdom. The different religious voices you are hearing may leave you uncertain about whom to believe. If this describes you, listen to what Jesus said in this encounter with the crowd.

The Convicted Seekers

A fourth group also would have been a part of this massive throng of people. These were people actually seeking to learn more about Jesus Christ and salvation. They had heard Him preach about the kingdom of God and were processing what Jesus had taught about the way of salvation. Among this part of the swelling numbers were individuals who were coming under the conviction of their sin. They were becoming acutely aware of their need for the grace of forgiveness that Jesus was offering.

These convicted seekers knew that what they had experienced in life to this point was nothing more than emptiness without God. A deep restlessness was provoking them to follow this new Teacher. They undoubtedly were being convicted that they fell short of the divine standard in the Law and persuaded that they did not measure up to what God required.

Painfully Aware

A loud alarm was sounding within their troubled consciences. They were painfully aware that something was not right between them and God. Something was missing. As they heard Jesus speak, they heard that they needed to commit their lives to Him. They learned they needed to respond to His free offer of the kingdom of God. But they had not yet received it by faith. They were not yet ready to make this commitment. The enormity of this decision was dawning upon them and they felt they could not walk away from their old ways. They stood at the crossroads of life.

This is precisely where many people are today. Perhaps even you. You know that whatever you have experienced to this point has not been the reality of the grace of God. You know the haunting conviction of your sin that will not go away and that you need the forgiveness that Jesus offers. Maybe you continue to follow with the religious crowd that gathers at church. Maybe you are a part of a small group Bible study. Or maybe you continue to talk about spiritual things with another person at work. But you have not yet made the decision to become an authentic follower of Christ. Could this describe where you are?

The Counterfeit Followers

In these large crowds, there was a fifth category of people. These are those who give the appearance of being genuine disciples. They were adept at blending in with the religious crowd and knew the right words to use to sound spiritual. They were adept at masking their own spiritual void. They enjoyed this close proximity to Jesus and even traveled with Him. They were not lagging behind Jesus at a distance, but were actually right next to Him.

In reality though, they were not authentic believers in Jesus Christ. They were merely caught up in the excitement of this movement. Truth be known, they had a superficial attachment to Jesus. They had an empty testimony in Christ. They professed a knowledge of Christ, but did not know Him personally in their hearts.

One Like Judas

One such follower who fit this description was a man named Judas. He was a charter member of the inner circle around Jesus. He was one of the twelve disciples who ate and lived with Jesus. Judas was as involved in ministry as anyone else, maybe even more so. He was privy to the inner workings of the work of the kingdom and observed firsthand the personal integrity in the life of Christ. He heard the profound truths that Jesus taught and witnessed with his own eyes the powerful miracles that Jesus performed. He saw the people whose lives had been dramatically transformed. He was so highly respected by the other eleven disciples that they made him the treasurer in charge of their money.

Yet despite all this advantage, Judas remained a counterfeit disciple. He had perfected the art of acting religious. He had a safe hiding place in the shadows of Jesus. But in his heart, he remained uncommitted to Christ. Judas had never died to self and he continued to pursue his own selfish interests. The chief pursuit of his life remained himself. He saw Jesus as a means for personal gain and had no desire in being sold out to Jesus. He wanted Jesus on his own terms. Tragically, Judas remained outside the kingdom of God. He had become so adept at looking religious that no one knew his hypocrisy. He even fooled himself.

Perhaps You?

Could this describe your life? Many people think of you as a Christian. But could it be that you are not? Maybe you grew up in a Christian home. Perhaps you have been baptized and joined the church. Maybe you regularly attend a Bible study. But could it be that you have never surrendered your life to Jesus Christ? Jesus demands that entering into His kingdom requires that you commit your entire life to Him. Have you done so?

Like Judas, could you be self-deceived about where you stand with God? There are large numbers of people who live under a false delusion regarding their spiritual state. Could you be one of these counterfeit converters?

Where Do You See Yourself?

These are much the same categories of people today who are going along with Jesus Christ. Nothing has changed over the centuries. This same diverse crowd is following Him with varying degrees of interest in what He has to say. Few are committed. Some are merely curious. Many are confused. Others are self-deceived.

Each one of us needs to ask ourselves, 'Where do I see myself in a gathering like this?' You need to examine yourself and determine where you are in your relationship to Jesus Christ. Where the different people were two thousand years ago is where each one of us will find ourselves today. Nothing has changed over the centuries. Let us consider each group more carefully.

A Right Diagnosis

In the medical world, it is said that a right diagnosis is half the cure. The same is true in the spiritual realm. It is absolutely imperative that you have the right diagnosis of where you stand with the Lord. If you are to be a genuine disciple, a right assessment of where your life stands in relationship to Jesus Christ is critical. You must know where you are before you can know what you need to do.

In the following chapters we will carefully analyze what is required to be a genuine follower of Jesus Christ. In the next chapter, we will discover what Jesus said is non-negotiable. But I must warn you that what you will read are strong words from the lips of the Lord. I hope you are sitting down.

SHOCKING WORDS

If anyone comes to Me, and does not
hate his own father and mother and
wife and children and brothers and
sisters, yes, and even his own life, he
cannot be My disciple
(Luke 14:26).

Jesus Christ was a straight-talker. He always told it like it is.
He never minced words or beat around the bush. Whatever
controversy surrounded His ministry, it was rarely because He
was misunderstood. The very opposite was usually the case.
Trouble followed Him because He was explicit in what He said.
His words were not hard to understand – just hard to swallow.

What Jesus said to this particular crowd would easily rank
among the most shocking words ever to come from His lips.

This jolting statement was one of the hardest hitting sayings He ever uttered. This abrasive assertion was one of the most demanding sayings He ever issued. These provocative words require a teachable spirit in order to receive them. When Jesus stopped to address this multitude, here is how He began: 'If anyone comes to Me, and does not hate his own father and mother and wife and children and brothers and sisters, yes, and even his own life, he cannot be My disciple' (v. 26). These are sobering words that the Lord spoke to the crowd that day.

Jesus maintained that those who would be His followers must hate those whom they love the most. Did we hear that right? The Lord claimed that following Him requires hating the very ones who brought them into the world. Can this be right? They must hate their own spouse to whom they have unconditionally pledged to support. They must hate their own children who bear their own resemblance. Did Jesus really say that? Then Jesus goes one step further and makes an even greater demand. This plunges yet deeper into their souls. Jesus added that anyone who would be His disciple must hate his or her own life. Say that again?

What Does This Mean?

What did Jesus mean by these seemingly harsh words? Does this not contradict so much else of what He taught? Does not the fifth commandment say that we are to honor our father and mother (Exod. 20:11)? Did not Moses write that we are to love our neighbor as we love ourselves (Lev. 19:18)? Did not Jesus command us to love our enemies (Matt. 22:39-40)? Did not Jesus Himself care for His own mother as He hung upon the cross (John 19:27)? Did not Paul issue the imperative that husbands are to love their wives as Christ loved the church (Eph. 5:25)? Does not the Bible maintain that if a man does not provide for the members of his own household, he is worse than an infidel (1 Tim. 5:8)?

The answer to each of these questions is a resounding yes. Without room for equivocation, the Bible gives a clear and positive affirmative to each of these questions.

A Right Interpretation

The challenge for us is to rightly interpret these provocative words spoken by Christ. How do we harmonize this statement with the rest of Scripture? How do we square these words with everything else that the Bible teaches? At first glance, this demand by Jesus seems to contradict the rest of the Bible. How are we to understand this hard saying of Jesus?

I want you to know that this apparent contradiction can be resolved. The riddle can be solved. But first, let us consider how the hard saying begins.

An Open Invitation to All

Jesus begins this invitation by saying: 'If anyone comes to Me' (v. 26). When He says 'anyone,' He extended this offer to everyone in the crowd. This was an open summons that He issued to all people under the sound of His voice. It was issued to everyone that day, regardless of their past. It went out to all, whether they were religious or irreligious, moral or immoral, cultured or uncouth. Here is the free offer of the gospel to everyone in the crowd. Jesus might as well have said, 'whosoever.' No one was excluded from this open-armed invitation.

This broad appeal issued by Christ to come and follow Him is still being extended down through the centuries, to us today. It is being offered to each person this very moment. You are being personally addressed and invited by Jesus Himself. So large-hearted is Christ that He is still calling individuals, from far and wide, to become His disciples.

The Savior Calls

This call to come to Jesus necessitated that those in this crowd take this decisive step of faith in order to come to Him. Simply put, they must commit their entire life to Him. To come to Christ is the same as placing their whole trust in Him. It means to transfer their reliance on their own efforts to Christ's righteousness in order to have a right standing before God. In another passage, Jesus said, 'I am the bread of life; he who *comes* to Me will not hunger, and he who *believes* in Me will never thirst' (emphasis mine, John 6:35). Here, we see that coming to Jesus is the same as believing in Him.

Elsewhere, Jesus said, 'If anyone is thirsty, let him *come* to Me and drink' (emphasis mine, John 7:37b). Just as a person would thirst for water, take it up to their mouth, and drink it, Jesus called the crowd to come to Him in order to receive eternal life. They must long for Him by faith, and receive Him into their souls. He alone can satisfy the deepest thirsting of their souls. One sip of Him will satisfy forever.

The Summons To All

On another occasion, Jesus issued a similar invitation when He said: 'Come to Me, all who are weary and heavy-laden, and I will give you rest. Take My yoke upon you and learn from Me, for I am gentle and humble in heart, and YOU WILL FIND REST FOR YOUR SOULS. For My yoke is easy and My burden is light' (Matt. 11:28-30). This summons requires that the one who comes to Christ must humble himself in order to come under His yoke. Our Lord is speaking with metaphorical language. As an ox would submit to the yoke of its master, one must come to Christ and yield to His lordship.

By this gospel invitation, Jesus called for those in the crowd to exchange their heavy load of sin for His light yoke of grace. Jesus is offering true rest for their weary hearts. He calls us to cease from our labors to earn salvation by our tireless efforts of self-righteousness. He invites us to come and rest in His saving work on our behalf.

The one who issues the call sets the terms for following Him. No one comes to Jesus on his or her own conditions. No one cuts their own deal with Christ. No one negotiates lower terms with the Master. There is no give and take between these two parties. The terms may be accepted or refused – but never altered. This requirement is fixed by Jesus Himself.

The Hate Jesus Loves

To the astonishment of the crowd, Jesus set the conditions extremely high. Christ emphatically states that if anyone comes to Him, he must hate those whom he loves the most. This word *hate* leaps off the page every time I read this. It is a word that sounds so harsh and offensive. This undoubtedly jolted those who first heard this. These provocative words demanded careful attention. Quite frankly, these words are too strong to be ignored.

By this stunning statement, Jesus addressed those personal relationships that are the most cherished. He spoke to those human bonds of affection where the deepest loyalties lie. He started with their family members who meant the most to them. He addressed those whom they love the most – their parents, spouse, children, and siblings. 'If anyone comes to Me and does not hate his own father and mother and wife and children and brothers and sisters, he cannot be My disciple.' What did Jesus mean?

An Intentional Exaggeration

As Jesus speaks, He is using a figure of speech known as hyperbole. This is an exaggerated statement that is intended to make a critical point. In this case, Jesus is deliberately setting love and hate in contrast to each other. He places them in juxtaposition as polar opposites. When Jesus says we must 'hate' our own family members, He actually means we must love them less than we love Him. He indicates that anyone who would follow Him must love Him more than the people closest to them. We must love Him more than anyone or anything in this world. If we are to be a true disciple of Christ, what we feel for others must appear to be as hate when compared to the greater devotion that we have for Him.

Scripture Interprets Scripture

This understanding is confirmed when we use Scripture to interpret Scripture. Jesus Christ Himself clarifies this perplexing statement elsewhere when He stated, 'He who loves father or mother more than Me is not worthy of Me; and he who loves son or daughter more than Me is not worthy of Me' (Matt. 10:37). Here, the words of Christ become crystal clear. We must love Jesus *more than* all others. This requires the commitment of one's entire life to Him. There can be no rival affections that compete with our love for Christ.

If we are to follow Christ, He must be our first priority and our most fervent passion. Jesus will not settle for second place in any of our lives. He says, 'Seek first His kingdom and His righteousness' (Matt. 6:33). Everything else in life is peripheral – Jesus is primary.

Mind, Affections, and Will

Loving Jesus Christ begins with our minds. We cannot love someone we do not know. We cannot love them until we know something about that person. Loving Christ begins with knowing who He is, what His character is, and what He has done, is doing, and will do. We need to learn what He said and taught. In order to love Jesus Christ, our minds must be filled with the true knowledge of Him. Our love for Christ will never be real in an intellectual vacuum. All love for Him starts with gaining a deeper knowledge about Him.

Further, love for Jesus Christ also requires that our heart be ignited with strong affections for Him. Our knowledge about Christ should stoke the flames of our passion for Him. As we learn about the person and work of the Lord Jesus Christ, our hearts should be enflamed with deep emotions for Him. How could they not be? Beholding the perfect holiness of Christ and observing His sacrificial love demonstrated at the cross should melt our hearts toward Him. No genuine follower of Christ can look at His sinless life and His saving work and be unmoved. Our relationship with Him should never be cold, clinical, or stoic. There has to be a fervent first-love for Christ that ignites our affections for Him.

Finally, any genuine love for Christ will also drive our will. Jesus said, 'If you love Me, you will keep My commandments' (John 14:15). This means our love for Christ should produce our obedience to Him. Wherever genuine love for Christ is the root, grace-fueled obedience will be the fruit.

A Full Commitment

Marriage is an accurate reflection of this reality. When I met my wife Anne, we initially got to know each other on an intellectual level. I first acquired an understanding of who and what she is. I learned about her life priorities, goals, and ambitions. There was a distinctly intellectual component in learning about her family background and life interests. An excitement level soon arose in my heart for her. I was drawn and emotionally excited to be with her. The growing depth of my affections for her compelled me to ask her to marry me. I pledged my life to her. As I stood at the front of the church on our wedding day, I chose to commit my life to her for the rest of my life.

This is a faint picture of what it is like to become a follower of Christ. It means that you come to love Him more than anyone or anything in life. You do more than merely know about Him. You come to know who He is and why He came. It means that you love and adore Him. You have committed your life to Him.

Hating Your Life

Jesus gave another provocative statement about following Him. With His next statement, His words revealed in a yet deeper way what is required to follow Him. Christ also added that each person must hate 'even his own life' (v. 26). These words mandate that we must love Christ far more than we even care for our own lives. A follower of Christ must die to self-love. We cannot remain self-focused, self-motivated, and self-reliant. We must love Him more than we love ourselves.

Jesus then issues this strong warning, 'or you cannot be My disciple.' A genuine follower of Jesus Christ cannot love himself supremely. For any authentic disciple, Christ must be the number one affection. This is the supreme loyalty that He requires. The supreme allegiance of any follower's life must be the Lord Jesus Christ. This level of commitment is absolutely necessary in order to be His disciple. Jesus does not want a mere place in our lives. He demands the preeminence.

Non-Negotiable Terms

If we are to be His disciple, this kind of supreme commitment to Christ is non-negotiable. It is easy to be merely in the crowd, tagging along behind Him. It is easy to be caught up in the high emotions of the multitude. But when Jesus addressed the crowd, He called for the total commitment of each person's life. Otherwise, He asserted, they cannot be His disciple. Jesus stated this in the negative so that His words will have a sharp edge to them. He meant to grab their attention and provoke their thinking.

To this day, Jesus continues to call individuals to Himself with this same demand. He is still calling us to love Him more than our own father and mother. The Lord continues to issue this summons to love Him more than our brother and sister. He is still inviting us to have a greater love for Him than for our own life.

I want to ask you: have you answered this invitation by Jesus Christ? Have you come all the way to Christ by faith? If not, what holds you back? What prevents you from loving Him more than anyone else?

No Fine Print

And He turned and said to them, 'If anyone comes to Me, and does not hate his own father and mother and wife and children and brothers and sisters, yes, and even his own life, he cannot be My disciple'
(Luke 14:25-26).

One thing was certain about the invitation Jesus issued to this crowd – there was no fine print in the terms. He did not hide the cost required in following Him. He never marked down the price tag for being His disciple. He never sought to manipulate anyone by lowering the terms. He never dumbed down the message. He never tried to induce a shallow decision from anyone. He never lowered the requirement to follow Him so that He could enlarge the crowds.

Jesus made the high cost of following Him clearly known. He announced on the front end what it would require. He let it be known to all listeners what the price was for being His disciple.

How different this is from the way that religious hucksters work. These charlatans are smooth-talking conmen. They are shell game specialists, sleight-of-hand magicians with words. They induce people to buy their message by withholding what Jesus said is the true cost. The high price of being a disciple is hidden, and they focus, instead, exclusively, upon the perks. They exaggerate what their hearers will gain, but never tell them what they must sacrifice. They fail to present the full price of a personal commitment to Christ.

Tragically, this is what so many people think following Jesus Christ is. They hear only about the benefits of forgiveness of sin. To them, Jesus is an ever-present genie in a bottle, always on call, always ready to grant to us our three wishes. They contemplate a home in heaven, but they never hear about the self-denial and sacrifice this will mean here on earth, much less about the suffering.

A Full Disclosure

Jesus was a frank, forthright truth-teller. He gave a full disclosure of what it would cost to follow Him. He was upfront with people. He understood that a genuine commitment can be made only if people know what it will cost them. This is why He told about the personal sacrifice required to be His disciple. He challenged them on the front end with the demands of discipleship.

Tragically, many individuals today give no thought what it will cost them to follow Jesus. It should come as no surprise to any of us that difficulty always accompanies the gospel. Look at what it cost Jesus to purchase our salvation. It will come with a cost factor for all who receive it. There was a cross for Jesus – there will be a cross for us. We must never become disillusioned when we suffer for our loyalty to Christ. Nothing has failed. Sure, we want the benefits from being identified with Him. Certainly, we want the provision and protection He gives. But we must not fail to recognize what it costs to be His disciple.

What Is A Disciple?

At this point, an important question needs to be raised – what is a disciple? The word disciple is a term used three times by Jesus in these few verses. It is the last word in verses 26, 27, and 33. The full reality of becoming a disciple is the central thrust of this discourse. Jesus wanted His followers to be fully devoted disciples. Jesus was never interested in merely attracting curiosity seekers for numbers' sake. He did not want to gather people who were simply highly interested observers of His ministry. Rather, He demanded fully-surrendered followers who submitted their entire beings to Him. Before Jesus ascended back to heaven, He commanded His disciples: 'Go, therefore, and make disciples of all the nations' (Matt. 28:19). In this charge, He stressed that He was seeking disciples, not empty decisions or passive spectators.

It would not be until years later that the early disciples were first called 'Christians' (Acts 11:26). Christian is the diminutive form for Christ, meaning a 'little Christ.' It was a word first dredged up by the world as a term of derision, intended to mock the early believers. By this name, these initial followers of Christ were being belittled for their connection with a crucified Jew considered to be public enemy number one. But these first believers embraced this taunt of association with their Master. They instead wore the name 'Christian' as a badge of honor. However, during the earthly ministry of Christ, these early believers were first called disciples by Jesus Himself.

A genuine disciple was a true believer in Jesus Christ. Today, the term disciple has come to mean something else. Unfortunately, it has been stripped of its original meaning. Presently, the word has been downgraded to represent anyone who attends a small group Bible study or someone who has a higher level of commitment. But as it was used by Jesus, the word disciple meant an authentic believer who was soundly converted to Him.

Under the Master

Given the importance assigned to being a disciple, it is critical that we know what the word means. It comes from a Greek word (*mathetes*) which means a learner or pupil. It was one who sat under the direct instruction of a master teacher. In ancient times, a rabbi – meaning teacher – was often an itinerant instructor who was followed by a small band of disciples. These students embraced his teaching and emulated his life. The rabbi would give his philosophy on life and teach on a broad range of topics. His followers would listen and adopt their rabbi's manner of thinking. It was a common sight to see such mobile classrooms in active session in the streets of the cities.

As it relates to being a disciple of Jesus Christ, it is one who has submitted his entire life to the teaching of Christ. In His earthly ministry, Jesus was often called rabbi, and His followers were His disciples. Being addressed as 'rabbi' (John 1:38, 49; 3:2; 4:32; 6:25; 9:2; 11:8) meant that He was recognized to be an authoritative teacher. His disciples were those who chose to recognize the authority of His teaching and surrendered to Him in order to follow and live out what He taught. Wherever Jesus went, He was surrounded by those who sat under the direct influence of His teaching.

During His days here, Jesus established a teacher-student relationship with those who followed Him. In simplest terms, a disciple was a learner and follower. He learned what Jesus taught and lived out what He instructed. This person obeyed His teaching – without active obedience, no one could be a true disciple.

Divine Truth Teacher

Throughout His ministry, Jesus claimed that His teaching was authoritative. He taught what He had directly received from His Father. He asserted: 'My teaching is not Mine, but His who sent Me' (John 7:16). That is, His teaching came with the divine authority of God Himself. Consequently, obedience to His teaching was direct obedience to God. Again He maintained: 'He who sent Me is true; and the things which I heard from Him, those I speak to the world...I do nothing on My own initiative, but I speak these things as the Father taught Me' (John 8:26, 28). Therefore, following what Jesus taught was actually obeying what God had taught. Jesus affirmed: 'I speak the things which I have seen with My Father' (John 8:38). What Jesus taught and passed on to His disciples, He received directly from God the Father.

Repeatedly, Jesus claimed solidarity between what He taught His disciples and what God had taught Him. 'For I did not speak on My own initiative, but the Father Himself who sent Me has given Me a commandment *as to* what to say and what to speak. I know that His commandment is eternal life; therefore the things I speak, I speak just as the Father has told Me' (John 12:49-50).

God Speaking

Again Jesus claims: 'The words that I say to you I do not speak on My own initiative, but the Father abiding in Me does His works' (John 14:10b). Jesus maintained that every truth He spoke was from the Father. Further, 'the word which you hear is not Mine, but the Father's who sent Me' (John 14:24b). A disciple clearly discerns the authoritative truth of God in the words of Christ.

A disciple of Christ was one who recognized that His teaching was not merely one more voice amid the many religious teachers in the world. Rather, a true disciple of Jesus realized that Jesus spoke the unparalleled wisdom of God. Whatever Jesus stated must be received as the final word from God on any subject. A disciple recognized that Jesus is the highest authority and final arbitrator on every matter. Whatever Jesus said is the way things truly are.

A disciple recognized the lordship of Christ and aligned his life under His teaching.

Teaching with Divine Authority

Being the Son of God, Jesus taught with infallible authority. Consequently, those who heard Jesus 'were amazed at His teaching; for He was teaching them as one having authority, and not as their scribes' (Matt. 7:28-29). The crowds who gathered around Him were 'astonished' and said, 'Where did this man get this wisdom?' (Matt. 13:54). All who heard Jesus recognized the profundity of His teaching.

The whole crowd was 'astonished at His teaching' (Mark 11:18). This means that His teaching blew their mind, so to speak. Even those who were sent to arrest Him returned empty-handed, mesmerized by His words saying, 'Never has a man spoken the way this man speaks' (John 7:46). Jesus exceeded any teaching they had ever heard. Again we read: 'They were astonished at His teaching' (Matt. 22:33). A genuine disciple was amazed at the teaching of Jesus Christ and chose to follow Him by living the reality of what He required.

A Learner Who Follows

Jesus made it clear that His true disciples are marked by obedience to His word. He declared: 'Not everyone who says to Me, "Lord, Lord," will enter the kingdom of heaven, but he who does the will of My Father who is in heaven' (Matt. 7:21). His genuine followers are those who live in obedience to the teaching of God. Jesus asked, 'Why do you call Me, "Lord, Lord," and do not do what I say?' (Luke 6:46). This rhetorical question implies a negative answer. Those who genuinely confess Jesus to be their Lord will show the validity of their claim by their lifestyle of obedience. It was not the perfection of their lives, but the direction of their lives, that was distinct.

Jesus emphatically said: 'If you continue in My word, then you are truly disciples of Mine' (John 8:31). True disciples are obedient to His word. But such obedience must come from a heart of love for Him. He said: 'If you love Me, you will keep My commandments.... He who has My commandments and keeps them is the one who loves Me' (John 14:15, 21a). A disciple of Christ is one who keeps His words out of love for the Savior. This is how we must live our lives.

The True Measure of Success

Unlike many today, Jesus Christ never measured the success of His ministry by the size of the crowd. He knew full well how easy it was to attract a full crowd of empty followers. Concealed in the multitude, Jesus knew that one could remain inconspicuous without making a genuine commitment to Him. He understood the magnetic pull of wanting to be in a crowd. Many people simply want to be wherever other people are, and nothing more. The bigger the crowd, the more others could be present without a real commitment.

To the contrary, the Lord desired a handful of genuine disciples who walked in obedience over a large number of observers who were unconverted. He was interested in the spiritual reality of the individuals attached to Him, not the numerical size or external appearance of the crowd.

A Discerning Gaze

Because of the superficiality in the crowd, Jesus did something that shocked His twelve disciples. He sized up the crowd and knew it had become a mixed bag of people. They were at different places in their spiritual life, some committed, many uncommitted. He peered into their hearts and discerned that a few were genuine disciples. But He saw that many were superficial attenders with no level of commitment to Him. As a result, Jesus stopped and turned around to address this multitude. He realized that it was becoming far too easy to merely tag along with Him.

In what He said, the Lord will make known the necessary requirements for being one of His true disciples. He will state what are the bare minimum prerequisites to be His disciple. As Jesus issued these words He called for the unconditional surrender of their lives to Him. Such resignation is the hallmark of a genuine disciple.

Still Shocking Today

Quite frankly, what Jesus said is still shocking to this day. The terms for following Him remain as demanding as when He spoke them. The high cost of being His disciple has never been marked down. Salvation is offered freely to all who will receive it. Jesus Christ paid the forgiveness of sins in full at the cross. He promises His saving grace as a free gift to those who do not deserve it. But if anyone is to receive it, he must humble himself in submission to His supreme authority.

These words spoken by Christ will negate any possibility of easy believism. No true disciple can live contrary to his confession of faith in Christ. This requires that we must determine if we are a genuine follower of Christ. If we have genuinely surrendered our life to Christ, there will be the reality of living for Christ for others to see. Throughout the journey of the Christian life, Jesus said: 'If anyone wishes to come after Me, he must deny himself, and take up his cross daily and follow Me' (Luke 9:23). There is no fine print here. In order to be a true disciple of Christ, you must make the decision to step out of the crowd and wholeheartedly follow Him.

Will you follow Jesus?

5
CROSS-BEARING

Whoever does not carry his own
cross and come after Me cannot be
My disciple (Luke 14:27).

Few statements that Jesus issued were ever more scandalous than what He said to this crowd. In no uncertain terms, Jesus said that anyone who would follow Him must carry his own cross. These words are hard for the modern mind to grasp. Such provocative teaching was intended to arrest the attention of His listeners. These were shocking words.

A Roman cross was considered an obscenity to the first century world. This form of capital punishment was reserved for only the most despicable criminals against the Roman Empire. In the ancient world, a cross was the most dreaded form of public execution. A cross was so offensive that no Roman citizen was allowed to suffer this barbaric death. Death by crucifixion was a slow, torturous death that prolonged the relief of death for the guilty offender.

Yet, here is Jesus saying to this crowd that those who would follow Him must take up their cross. These sobering words shocked the sensibilities of those in the crowd. Christ meant to jolt their thinking. He intended to penetrate their conscience. These stunning words are as follows: 'Whoever does not carry his own cross and come after Me cannot be My disciple' (Luke 14:27).

An Open Invitation

In this verse, Jesus reissued the same invitation He had just previously extended. This demanding summons began with the open invitation, 'whoever.' This all-inclusive 'whoever' parallels the 'anyone' in the preceding verse. No matter who they were, or whatever they had done, they were invited by Jesus to respond to this appeal. 'Whoever' is wide enough to include anyone and everyone in the crowd. This open appeal was extended to all in this vast multitude that day. Regardless of their social background, no matter what their moral failures had been, all were invited by this summons to follow Him. By saying 'whoever,' Jesus swung open the door leading into the kingdom of God. The gates of Paradise were unlocked to allow all who would come to gain entrance.

This same open invitation by Jesus was extended many times. He said: 'Enter by the narrow gate' (Matt. 7:13).

This invitation is broad in its scope. All who hear it should come at once. It does not matter how far removed from God a person's life may be. All are invited by Christ to come to Him. Jesus will receive you. In His own day, Jesus was criticized. Others condemned Him, saying 'This man receives sinners' (Luke 15:2). Yet Jesus said: 'the one who comes to Me I will certainly not cast out' (John 6:37). He says, 'If anyone is thirsty, let Him come to Me and drink' (John 7:37). It does not matter how far short your life has fallen from what God requires it to be. Jesus invites you to come and extends His undeserved grace.

It does not matter where you come from in life. It does not matter how you have lived in the past. It does not matter how sinful your present may be. Jesus is the Great Physician of the soul. He has not come into the world for those who are well. He has come for the sick and, your sin is no hindrance for Him to receive you.

The Terms of Acceptance

While extending this open invitation, Jesus also set the necessary conditions for following Him. Jesus said: 'whoever does not carry his own cross...cannot be My disciple.' This statement contains a double negative. Twice in this one verse Jesus says 'not.' This makes His words doubly pointed and especially emphatic. Cross bearing is mandatory for all who would answer this invitation. Here is the necessity that if anyone is to follow Christ, that person must carry his or her own cross. By these words, Jesus was not talking about wearing a piece of gold jewelry around one's neck. No one in the crowd would have misunderstood it that way.

In the first century, the cross was an instrument that inflicted the cruelest death. It was the most feared form of capital punishment in that day. The cross was the equivalent of the electric chair of the ancient world. It meant a horrific death that unleashed the most excruciating pain possible. Death by crucifixion was so barbaric that it was reserved for the worst criminals of society. Only terrorists, insurrectionists, anarchists, robbers, thieves and the like were hung upon crosses.

The Death March

The proceedings would unfold as follows. An accused criminal would stand trial before a judge who had the power of life and death in his hands. If the accused was found guilty of a capital crime, he would be sentenced to death by crucifixion. The criminal would be forced to carry his crossbar through the streets of the city to the execution site on the outskirts of town. This was known as the death march and was a public display of his guilt before everyone. It was intended to bring public shame. Carrying one's cross was considered an agreement with the judge's death sentence. It was forced admission of guilt under the law and an agreement with the verdict of the higher court.

As the criminal carried his crossbeam, the people of the city would line both sides of the streets. This was meant to be a public spectacle. It graphically signified that this offender was condemned by Rome and worthy of death. This individual was considered to be a dead man walking. It would be upon this very crossbeam that the criminal would be nailed in the act of crucifixion and lifted up to die.

A Necessary Requirement

By this humiliating death march, Jesus is stating that those who follow Him must assume the very same posture, spiritually speaking. They must see themselves as standing before the judgment of God having been found guilty of breaking His moral law. They have been weighed in the balances and been found to be wanting. Understanding this means agreeing with the divine verdict of the heavenly court.

Those who would follow Christ must see themselves in need of God on a daily basis. They must turn to Jesus Christ in repentance and faith. As a believer, they must carry their cross daily. This means that the ones who would follow Christ must not rely on themselves any longer, but solely on Him. They must live daily looking to Jesus for strength and direction.

Coming After Jesus

When Jesus invited the crowd to come *after* Him, He was not talking in literal terms. He was not requiring that these individuals take physical steps along the dusty road upon which He was walking. Jesus is speaking in metaphorical terms. The meaning was for the crowd to take a decisive step of faith within their hearts. The call was to come to Him by their faith, not by their feet.

By this analogy, cross-bearing represented a personal allegiance to Christ. If anyone is to follow Him, they must carry their cross in this world. Jesus will not follow them. Instead, they must follow Him. He will not do what they want, they must do what He commands. Which also means they must follow Him in the manner that He prescribes.

The same is true for everyone who would follow Christ today. Cross-bearing is necessary for every person who would come after Him. No one can follow Jesus *and* continue to live in the same way as they did previously. To follow Christ, means you must do a complete turnaround from the direction you were previously traveling in life. Before you chose to follow Christ, you were walking according to the course of this world (Eph. 2:3). You were headed toward destruction. In order to follow Christ, you must go in an entirely different direction. You must carry your cross and look to Him.

An Urgent Appeal

As Jesus extended this invitation, He did so in an urgent manner. Jesus was not casual or laid back about this appeal to come to Him. He was not lackadaisical in the tone of His voice. He did not adopt a take it or leave it attitude. Instead, He pressed upon those in the crowd that day to respond to His invitation now. This was not something that could be delayed. They could not postpone responding. They were not given the latitude to address other concerns first. They were not extended the option to pursue other interests over this one. This was the most important decision before them and had to be answered immediately.

Responding to this invitation is the priority for every person. This call cannot be put off. It cannot be moved down your list of pressing things. Answering this invitation is the single most important issue in your life. It must be addressed and answered now.

Now Is The Time

The entire Bible speaks to the urgency of choosing to take up your cross and carrying it now. 'Behold, now is "THE ACCEPTABLE TIME" behold, now is "THE DAY OF SALVATION"' (2 Cor. 6:2). The word 'now' indicates the present urgency in coming to faith in Christ. Refusing to respond to this invitation immediately is a serious matter because of what is on the line. The Bible says: 'Do not boast about tomorrow, For you do not know what a day may bring forth' (Prov. 27:1). Waiting to make a delayed decision for Christ is a dangerous postponement. You have no idea if you will have the time tomorrow with which to make this decision as you do today.

A Lifelong Decision

The decision to carry your cross is the one you must make. If you decide not to decide, that is itself a decision not to follow Christ. Your decision to carry your cross means death to your old way of life. It marks the beginning of an entirely new way of life. You must carry your cross every step of life's journey for the rest of your life. To carry your cross is not a one-time act at the beginning of following Christ. Cross-bearing must be a daily experience and will continue the entirety of your life.

You must step out of the crowd to follow Christ. You must travel down this new path. There must be a willingness to go wherever Jesus sends you. You must do whatever He calls you to do. Or you cannot be His disciple.

These are strong words. But these strong words by Christ make strong disciples who have strong faith.

FOLLOWING JESUS (I)

Whoever does not carry his own
cross and come after Me cannot be
My disciple (Luke 14:27).

The greatest invitation ever issued is the one extended to us
by Jesus Christ in the gospel. It is an open appeal to all who
hear His voice to respond by coming to Him. Jesus issued
many such appeals to crowds throughout His public ministry. He repeatedly and personally called people to come
and commit their lives to Him.

Among these many petitions, the one most frequently given
was the call to follow Him. Thirteen times in the four Gospels

we read these words 'Follow Me.' This is exactly what Jesus is saying through this call, yet in slightly different words. When He invites them to 'come after Me,' He is saying 'Follow Me.'

By this summons, Jesus was not enlisting people to join a social cause. Neither was He recruiting people to sign up for a religious movement. He was not signing people up to a political group. The invitation issued by Jesus was a call for individuals to follow Him in a personal relationship.

Let us now consider the various aspects of this powerful call. To answer it requires the commitment of the individual to Jesus Christ. What kind of commitment is required? In this chapter I want to designate six aspects of this commitment that are either stated or implied in this call. In the next chapter, we will continue our consideration of this with five more marks.

A Priority Commitment

First, Jesus was calling each person to follow Him *preeminently*. No other call they would ever hear would take precedence over this one. Answering this call was the number one priority they had in life. This call jumped to the head of the list for what was most critical in their life. Nothing could overshadow this call. Answering this call issued by Jesus would be the most important decision of their life.

The significance of this appeal was found in the One who was calling them. Issuing this invitation was the Lord Jesus Christ, the One sent by God from heaven. Summoning them was the One sent to rescue them from the wrath to come. Voicing this call was the One who was validated by God as the Messiah sent to deliver them from their sins. This One speaking to them had restored sight to the blind, hearing to the deaf, functioning limbs to the lame and health to the sick. The One inviting them had raised the dead back to life. They must listen to this One who alone can speak peace to the raging storms. They must give Him their undivided attention and respond by faith.

The same is true for you and me today. The call of Jesus upon our lives remains the most important issue confronting us. Nothing takes precedence over this summons. Answering it is the top priority in our lives. Have you responded by faith to His invitation?

A Personal Commitment

Second, Jesus was calling each person to follow Him *personally*. Each person in that vast sea of humanity was required to make this decision for themselves. No one else could respond for them. Their spouse could not answer it for them. Their friends could not choose to respond on their behalf. Though they were standing in the midst of a large multitude, this could not be a group decision. Jesus was requiring that each individual person search their own heart and respond to this truth. Each person had to exercise their own will to follow Him. He was calling for a personal relationship with Him, not a collective one.

Earlier, Jesus had asserted: 'Enter through the narrow gate' (Matt. 7:13). This gate represents the conversion that leads into the kingdom of God. This gate is so narrow that it prohibits an entire group of people to pass through it. There is room for only one person at a time to pass through its narrow confines. Everyone who comes to Christ must come to Him individually.

So it is for each one of us. This is the personal decision that we must make individually to follow Christ. No one else can make this commitment for us. Our husband or wife cannot do this for us. This is not even a decision that our pastor or spiritual leader can make for us. It must be *our* choice to follow Christ that requires the exercise of *our* will. We must own this relationship with Christ for ourselves.

A Repentant Commitment

Third, Jesus called those in this multitude to follow Him *repentantly*. Those in the crowd had to stop walking according to the course of this world. They had to do a reverse pivot and turn around in order to walk towards Him. They had to turn their backs to the practice of sin and the pollution of the world. They had to forsake their old ways of life. They could no longer live for themselves. They could no longer run after the sin they once pursued. They must resist the self-centered focus by which they had been previously operating and forsake the broad path of the world.

The call that Jesus issued was a call to repentance. Jesus began His public ministry by saying: 'Repent, for the kingdom of heaven is at "hand"' (Matt. 4:17). He announced: 'Repent and believe in the gospel' (Mark 1:15). In order to follow Jesus there had to be repentance – a godly sorrow over one's own sin and the turning away from it to follow Him.

Repentance is absolutely necessary to follow Jesus. He is the holy, sinless Son of God. He has never walked in sin or even pursued unholy pleasures. Those whom He calls to follow Him must turn their backs on their sin and renounce the evil world's system. They must set their faces toward the pursuit of personal holiness. No one can follow Christ without abandoning their former life of sin.

Those unconverted in the large crowds were traveling the broad path. This spacious path was wide enough to accommodate their sinful lifestyles. This expansive path could permit any manner of living they chose and tolerate any standard of morality they desired. To follow Christ, they must exit this path if they are to enter the narrow path to eternal life. This is the true repentance that Jesus demanded.

This requirement of true repentance remains the same for us today. This necessity of turning away from living in sin remains in effect. Following Christ necessitates that you turn away from the sinful path you once traveled. Coming after Jesus means that you renounce your sinful past. It requires you travel down an entirely new path of following Jesus in a sanctified life.

A Trusting Commitment

Fourth, Jesus was calling them to follow Him *believingly*. That is to say, this decision to follow Christ necessitated that you come to Him by faith. When Jesus issued this call, He did not tell those in the crowd where this would take them. Neither did He tell them what all would be required. He did not explain who else would be joining them. Their singular requirement was to follow Him. Whether the whole crowd would come, or no one else would come, their singular responsibility was to follow Him.

This call required that they trust Jesus for everything. This begins by looking to Him for salvation. By this commitment, they rely upon Him solely for a right standing before God. They must be dependent upon Him to deliver them from the wrath of God which they deserve. They needed to believe in Him to rescue them from the just punishment of their sins, and attach themselves to Him to receive His forgiveness and righteousness.

A Wholehearted Commitment

Fifth, Jesus called those in the crowd to come after Him *wholeheartedly*. To answer this call, these individuals had to step out of the crowd and fully align with Him as His disciples. They could not hold back any part of their life from Him. They could not be half in, and half out with Him. They could not come to Him and still remain with the crowd. Their entire life must be surrendered to Him, or they could not be His true disciples.

No one could follow Christ with a divided heart. Jesus addressed this wholehearted commitment when He said: 'No one can serve two masters; for either he will hate the one and love the other, or he will be devoted to one and despise the other. You cannot serve God and wealth' (Matt. 6:24). This meant that no one could be His true follower and still remain committed to this world and its desires. This call demanded an all or nothing response. No one could ride the fence. They could not play all ends into the middle. If they were to follow Christ, they must be entirely devoted to Him. Being a disciple of Jesus meant that He must be their all-consuming priority, passion and pursuit in life.

Nothing Has Changed

This same wholehearted commitment is still required today. Nothing has changed. Jesus will not accept a mere peripheral place in our lives. He demands the primary preeminence. There cannot be a divided loyalty in our hearts. We cannot follow Him *and* something else. We cannot follow Christ *and* pursue this world. We cannot love our family or job more than we love Him. We cannot run after earthly pleasures more than we desire to pursue Him. If we are to truly follow Him, Jesus must be our greatest passion and pleasure.

By this call, Jesus is demanding our total allegiance to Him. This mandates the unhindered response of our entire being and a surrender of our entire life to Him. Is this where you are? Is this the kind of commitment you have made to Him? If not, do you need to make this decisive entrustment to Him? If we are to follow Him, we must be all in with Jesus. It is too important a decision to respond halfheartedly.

An Unconditional Commitment

Sixth, Jesus called those in the crowd to follow Him *unconditionally*. He summoned them to follow Him no matter what it would require, no matter where it would take them. Jesus urged the multitude to come after Him without any further explanation. Regardless of what difficulties lay ahead, they must come after Him. Regardless of what affliction this would mean, regardless of what persecution awaited them, they must follow Him.

There were to be no conditions placed on this commitment. Whatever it would take to fulfill His requirements was what they had to give. There could be no disciple who said to Christ, others, or himself: 'I will only go here to serve the Lord, but never there.' There could be no boundaries placed on where a follower of Christ would advance. A believer could not set limitations on what he would do for Christ, for no sacrifice is too great to make for Him who gave us His very life.

It is the same for anyone who would follow Christ today. All who would come after Him must have similar trust in Him and in His direction. You may not presently know where this journey will take you. Nor what it will require of you or even who will travel this path with you. Jesus does not provide us with details and itineraries. There is no promise of an easy life. Our entire journey must be lived by trusting our new master, Jesus Christ. And though we may not know the future or what it holds, we can trust our Savior who suffered on the cross to redeem His elect.

We must suffer any hardship for Him. We must be willing to go anywhere, do anything, and pay any price. He has paid the ultimate price on the cross, we can respond to this great love with this lesser sacrifice.

Where It Begins

With these first six marks of coming after Christ, this is what a true commitment involves. To summarize, this call to follow Him requires that you personally choose to commit your life to Jesus Christ. No one else can do this for you. Such an individual choice necessitates our wholehearted commitment to Him. You cannot be half in and half out with Christ. This decision requires that you repent of your sins and turn away from pursuing a life of self and turn to Christ. Moreover, you must do this unconditionally. There are no strings attached and no escape clauses in the fine print.

Are you ready to make this kind of commitment to Jesus Christ? Be assured, He is ready to receive you.

FOLLOWING JESUS (II)

Whoever does not carry his own
cross and come after Me cannot be
My disciple (Luke 14:27).

The Christian life is all about loving, knowing and following Jesus Christ. Being a genuine disciple means living in a personal relationship with Him. It involves believing in Jesus and following Him throughout one's entire life. It includes worshiping and adoring Him with all of one's heart. It is treasuring Him above all else. It leads to serving Him with one's entire being. Simply put, the Christian life is Christ.

Many confuse being a genuine Christian with merely being in church or being part of a religious group. But the reality of being a follower of Christ runs far deeper. The essence of being a disciple concerns itself not with where a person is physically, but where they are spiritually. Christianity is not following a mere cause or a code of conduct, but Christ Himself. This is the central truth that Jesus was establishing with this crowd. Each individual must not merely know about Him, but actually know Him personally.

This is what you and I desperately need to experience. We must know Jesus and become His disciple. This is a personal decision that can only take place in your heart. And from this decision and commitment will flow a great love and desire to worship Him. In an exercise of our will, we choose to follow Him above all else.

In this chapter we will continue what we began to examine in the previous chapter. We have already noted the first six aspects of how we must follow Christ. We must come after him preeminently, personally, repentantly, believingly, wholeheartedly and comprehensively. Here are six more distinguishing marks of following Christ. Let us now consider each one, beginning with the seventh mark.

An Obedient Commitment

Seventh, this call issued by Jesus required those in the crowd to follow Him *obediently*. This meant that they were to live their lives in obedience to His word. The words 'follow Me' are in the imperative mood and given as a command. This call is more than an invitation or free offer to be accepted or rejected. It is a command that must be obeyed or else it is disobedience. All true faith in Jesus is obedient faith. The moment one of them chose to follow Christ, they responded with a step of obedience.

In the Gospel of John, we read that believing in Jesus and obeying Him are used synonymously: 'He who believes in the Son has eternal life; but he who does not obey the Son will not see life, but the wrath of God abides on him' (John 3:36). In this verse, believing in Jesus and obeying Him cannot be separated. To believe in Him is to obey Him. Jesus said: 'Why do you call Me, "Lord, Lord," and do not do what I say?' (Luke 6:46). This rhetorical question implies a negative answer. No disciple can live in prolonged, habitual disobedience to His word. Jesus also said: 'If you continue in My word, then you are truly disciples of Mine' (John 8:31). Wherever there is saving faith, there will be a habitual lifestyle of obedience to the word of Christ. Obedience does not save you but it is evidence that true salvation has taken place.

Slaves of Righteousness

The identifying mark of true disciples is obedience to what God commands in His word. God has given the Holy Spirit 'to those who obey Him' (Acts 5:32). The apostle Paul maintains that every person lives a life of obedience. Either one lives in obedience to sin or in obedience to Jesus. He writes:' Do you not know that when you present yourselves to someone as slaves for obedience, you are slaves of the one whom you obey, either of sin resulting in death, or of obedience resulting in righteousness? But thanks be to God that though you were slaves of sin, you became obedient from the heart to that form of teaching to which you were committed' (Rom. 6:16-17). The point is, everyone lives in obedience to his or her master. Either a person lives under the governing power of sin or of Jesus. You either obey Christ, a loving and righteous master or obey sin, which enslaves you and brings only death and destruction.

The Bible says that Jesus is the source of salvation to 'all those who obey Him' (Heb. 5:9). Those who submit to the authority of God's word and keep it are those who reveal that they are saved. Peter states that those who believe the gospel 'obey Jesus Christ' (1 Pet. 1:2). The Scripture also states: 'By this we know that we have come to know Him, if we keep His commandments' (1 John 2:3). Those who truly know God in a saving relationship are those who live in obedience to Him. Saving faith always begins with obedience: 'This is His commandment, that we believe in the name of His Son Jesus Christ' (1 John 3:23). For the true believer, 'His commandments are not burdensome' (1 John 5:2-3) because they are a delight to keep.

An Open Commitment

Eighth, this call by the Lord to the crowd necessitated that they follow Him *openly*. They must live out their allegiance to Him before the watching eyes of this hostile world. They must give an open, public testimony of their loyalty to Him. Jesus made this clear: 'For whoever is ashamed of Me and My words in this adulterous and sinful generation, the Son of Man will also be ashamed of him when He comes in the glory of His Father with the holy angels' (Mark 8:38). In other words, they must unashamedly make known their relationship with Him. They must not conceal from the world that they are one of His disciples.

The apostle Paul announced: 'For I am not ashamed of the gospel, for it is the power of God for salvation to everyone who believes, to the Jew first and also to the Greek' (Rom. 1:16). By putting this in the negative he is making a powerful statement of his desire to make an open testimony of the gospel. The apostle is saying that he is ready to preach the gospel in Rome, the hardest city in the known world to gain a reception for this message. This is what following Christ requires. We must openly proclaim Him before all. We are to be 'speaking the truth in love' (Eph. 4:15). Also: 'Let your speech always be with grace, as though seasoned with salt' (Col. 4:6). We are called to be a faithful witness for Christ with grace and patience toward unbelievers.

Such an open witness for Christ is required for each one of us who follow Christ. We cannot walk with Him and be silent concerning to whom our allegiance belongs. It is our responsibility to openly testify for Him. As God gives opportunities, we must tell others about Christ.

A Continual Commitment

Ninth, Jesus called those in the crowd to follow Him *continually*. Christ stated 'come after Me' in the present tense. This means that those in the crowd must follow Jesus constantly every moment of every day. On the part of a disciple, this would be a daily lifestyle of coming after Him. This would not be reserved for only Sundays and they could live otherwise throughout the week. There would never be a moment of the day, month, or year when they would not be following Him.

They were to follow Jesus in good times and in bad times. They would follow Him in days of prosperity and in seasons of adversity. They would never take a day off from following Him. There would never be a sabbatical from following Him. No matter who they were with, no matter where they found themselves, they were to be living for Christ – in season and out of season, when it was convenient and when it was inconvenient, when it was accepted and when it was unaccepted.

Jesus said elsewhere that those who come after Him must do so 'daily' (Luke 9:23). This commitment is not a one time event, but an ongoing reality. This decision will lead to an every day, all day, habitual lifestyle.

An Exclusive Commitment

Tenth, Jesus called those in the crowd to follow Him *exclusively*. That is to say, they must come after Him only. They could not follow Him *and* the dead religion of Judaism. They could not follow Him *and* the mangled teaching of the Pharisees. They could not follow Him *and* the traditions of the Samaritans. They could not come after Him *and* any self-styled religion. They must follow Him and Him alone.

Jesus must be their sole source of truth. They cannot look to Him and to the wisdom of the world. They cannot come after Him *and* the ways of the Romans or the Greeks. They must follow the teaching of Jesus Christ exclusively. He must be to them *the* way, *the* truth, and *the* life. He could not be one more voice amid the many teachers competing for their attention. They must make the commitment to follow Jesus and no one else.

A Permanent Commitment

Eleventh, those whom Jesus called were required to come after Him *permanently*. Making this decision meant that there was no turning back to their former ways. He was not calling for a short-term commitment that could eventually be terminated. Jesus did not ask for a momentary following. He was calling for a long-term agreement in a new direction. This was a lifelong commitment that would guide their every step the rest of the way in life. Once the decision was made, their allegiance would always be to Him.

Jesus said: 'No one, after putting his hand to the plow and looking back, is fit for the kingdom of God' (Luke 9:62). This statement means that no one could plow a straight furrow while looking backwards. They must remain with their shoulder to the plow, looking forward. In like manner, no one can be a disciple of Christ who is constantly second-guessing himself whether he made the right decision to follow Christ. He cannot move forward with a divided heart. A genuine disciple will not desire to return to where they previously were before beginning this journey. Jesus stated that such a person is not fit for the kingdom of God because he was holding on to his past life.

This same prolonged commitment to follow Christ is required of us today. Once this decision is made, we cannot go back. There is to be no reversal of our life pursuit. There can be no escape clause that would allow us to retreat to our former manner of life and our old desires and sins. There is no ninety-day return policy for taking back the cross we bear. Following Christ is a lifelong commitment. This decision to follow Christ is not the start of a short sprint, but a long marathon. Do you see the depth and duration of a commitment required to follow Jesus?

An Immediate Commitment

Twelfth, when Jesus called those within this crowd, they were to respond *immediately*. There was a present urgency about answering this invitation that very moment. Following Christ was not a decision that could be postponed. The need was now. Other matters would have to wait. Life was too short for this to be deferred. Death was looming before them and eternity only a heartbeat away. This call must be answered straight away before it is too late.

The same is true for you. The gospel call still demands an immediate response from those who hear it. Jesus said: 'While you have the Light, believe in the Light, so that you may become sons of Light' (John 12:36). There is a limited time for us to believe in Christ. We must respond while the light of the knowledge of the gospel is shining. Whenever Jesus calls, there is an urgency to respond immediately.

Do Not Delay

Jesus is extending His call to you now. Do not delay to answer Him. He desires that you come to Him in faith and follow Him now. You must respond to His call while there is time.

Have you recognized your need to answer His call? Will you step out of the crowd and follow Him? Will you come to Him by faith? I urge you to do so now.

COUNTING THE COST

For which one of you, when he wants to build a tower, does not first sit down and calculate the cost to see if he has enough to complete it? Otherwise, when he has laid a foundation and is not able to finish, all who observe it begin to ridicule him, saying, 'This man began to build and was not able to finish' (Luke 14:28-30).

Anything worthwhile in life comes with a cost involved. There is always a personal sacrifice that is required with possessing something valuable. This is true whether it is succeeding in work, enjoying marriage, advancing in sports, or excelling with a musical instrument. Wherever there is no pain, there is no gain.

Nowhere is this truer than in the matter of following Jesus. Salvation is offered to us as a free gift from God.

But receiving it always comes at a high price. There are no exceptions to this truth. Granted, the price to be paid for being a Christian is higher for some than for others. We are born into different families, in different places and at different times in history. The price for our faith in Christ will differ from one person to the next, but there will always be a price to pay for all who come after Jesus.

Therefore, those in the crowd must count the cost of following Jesus before they make the commitment. If not, they could potentially make a superficial decision proving to be disingenuous. This is so important, in fact, that Jesus says it calls for a sober calculation. No one just decides this on a whim. The stakes are too high. It requires too much of you. Jesus calls every one of us to make a sober calculation in our own minds and hearts.

Back-to-Back Parables

In order to establish this point, Jesus told the crowd two parables in consecutive order. A parable is an earthly story with a heavenly meaning. These two stories were given back-to-back in order to communicate the same basic point. The crowd needs to know the cost before they follow Him. These two parables fit perfectly together – they are the heads and tails of the same coin.

In the first parable, Jesus explained that if anyone in the crowd chooses to follow Him, they must first calculate the cost. The second parable gives the other side of the coin. If they choose *not* to follow Christ, the result will be nevertheless the same. It will still cost them everything. A failure to commit their life to Him will cost them to suffer the eternal destruction of their soul. Whether they commit their life to Him or whether they choose to reject Him, it will cost them *everything*.

Since these words were first issued, this price tag has never been reduced. These demanding terms as set by our Lord remain the same for each person today who desires to follow Him. This includes you. This choice will affect your life for as long as you live. It will even determine your eternal destiny. Be careful to count the cost.

A Probing Question

The first parable that Jesus told began by asking that very question: 'For which one of you, when he wants to build a tower, does not first sit down and calculate the cost to see if he has enough to complete it?' (v. 28). When Jesus raised this question, He was looking squarely into the eyes of this vast crowd with the intention of provoking their thinking. He sought to challenge them to honestly assess their relationship to Him.

By this probing question, Jesus was provoking them to undergo serious soul-searching in regards to their spiritual state. Where do they stand with Him? Christ intended to respond positively to the call He issued. But they must first count the cost of discipleship. He wanted to capture the attention of those who were merely curious about His notoriety. He desired to secure the commitment of those who were simply caught up in the excitement of this movement. This was an evangelistic plea He was giving.

Calculating the Cost

This illustration drew upon a common life experience of a builder and a construction site. Any good builder would first count the cost of construction before entering into a building project. A wise builder would never be so foolish as to begin to build without first calculating the total cost. It would be shortsighted and ill-advised to rush into any construction project without, first, knowing what its total cost would be. The reason was simple enough. If he does not know the expense involved, he would discover too late and possibly be unable to complete this undertaking, he may be forced to abandon the project after wasting valuable time, money, and effort, to say nothing of his reputation.

In this parable, Jesus continued: 'Otherwise when he has laid a foundation, and is not able to finish all who observe it begin to ridicule him' (v. 29). What this builder started, he cannot finish. Why? Because he failed to count the cost on the front end. All started well. The ground has been prepared for construction. The trees were cleared out, the foundation built up, and the front door set in place. All was proceeding well, that is, until the project unexpectedly came to a standstill. No further building occurred. No more walls were erected, no more rooms were framed, and no roof was laid over the structure.

As the people of the town walked past this unfinished project, they mocked him. They laughed at him. But this laughter was not that of humor, but derision. He has become a public spectacle that suffers embarrassment before the entire town.

The Foolish Builder

The observers of this unfinished project would have concluded, 'This foolish builder must have failed to do a cost estimate.' They rightly surmised that everything spent on this project was wasted. Sadly, everyone in town knew it. This imprudent builder would be too ashamed to show his face. He would be the object of scorn by everyone as the irresponsible man who started this building project, but was unable to finish because he had not counted the cost.

How reckless it would be for this builder to realize too late that the cost was too high. The same would be for an imprudent man who would painfully discover that he could not complete what he started. Sadly, he would lose everything he had invested into the project. How humiliating and shameful it would be to walk away from the building project after he had started it. His only recourse would be to withdraw from the construction work. All would be lost.

A Superficial Decision

This parable symbolized those in the crowd who were superficial followers of Christ. Such people had never counted the cost of what this would really require from them. They were drawn in by the excitement of the crowd and the energy of the movement. They were interested in what Jesus taught about certain topics but they never considered the ultimate cost and sacrifice. Consequently, there was no real commitment to Him. How easy it was to jump into the crowd and begin the journey. But how hard it would be to finish. How effortless it was to launch this project, yet how costly it would be to complete it.

Countless people are like this today. They appear to start well in following Jesus. Maybe they start attending church. Perhaps they are inspired to get involved. Possibly moved by the hospitality being shown to them. All this makes them feel good. As a result, they make a hasty decision to repeat a prayer with a pastor. They join the church. They participate in a few spiritual activities, and go through various religious motions. But, tragically it is all external and they never genuinely come to know Jesus.

Abandoned Building Projects

Like the builder in the parable, this impetuous person appears to start so well. But old friends soon come around again. Old temptations return. Old habits reemerge. He meets some persecution for his religious association. He falls back into his former way of life. Sadly, he never comes back to church. This person is like this man in the parable who began to build, but was unable to finish due to the high cost.

This parable represents a vast number of people today. They hear the truth of the saving message of Jesus Christ. They want the benefits of salvation. They desire the peace of mind from knowing their sins are forgiven. They long for a home in heaven. But they give no thought to making a deep commitment to Christ. They are unwilling to give up the control of their life. They never considered a life lived like this. So, when it comes down to making a commitment, they walk away from the crowd that was following Christ.

Never Counted the Cost

Sadly, this person was never a true disciple. They did not lose their salvation, they never truly had it. Though they gave the appearance of being a follower of Christ, they had never counted the true cost of being His disciple. They were never an authentic disciple. The eventual falling away from Christ revealed that they never had exercised true saving faith from the beginning.

Any genuine commitment to Christ requires counting the cost before coming to Him. What will it cost you to follow Christ? It will cost you a life in which you choose your own way. It will cost you the freedom to do your own thing. It will cost you a life of ease. It will require that you live for God now and what He wants for you. You must burn your bridges behind you. There is no turning back.

It Will Cost You

What does it cost to be a disciple of Christ? It will cost us our self-righteousness. We can no longer consider ourselves to be a good person but rather a sinner who has broken God's laws. We are under the sentence of divine wrath and condemnation. Are we willing to pay that price? We must count the cost of forsaking the sins that we now cherish. We must abandon them for the things of the Lord that truly give life.

We must count the cost of giving up our own views about what life is all about. We must count the cost of forsaking friendship with the world and acknowledge that though we are in the world, we are not of the world. We must count the cost of foregoing our own plans for our lives in order to follow God's will. We have to count the cost of letting go of our own will for our lives.

Following Christ may cost you popularity with your old friends. It may cost you business success. It may cost you the applause of this world. Nothing in your life lies outside this commitment to Jesus Christ. You must think carefully about what this commitment requires. Otherwise, a rash decision to follow Christ that may fizzle out before the finish. You must count this cost.

Be assured that religion that costs nothing is worth nothing—and accomplishes nothing. Religion that costs you neither time nor thought, nor self-denial, nor sacrifice, nor prayer, nor suffering, nor opposition, nor persecution, nor conflict, will be a religion that will never save your soul. It is a religion that will give you no comfort in the day of adversity. It is a religion that will give you no peace in the day of your death.

More Gains Than Losses

Having issued this caution, let me remind you that what you gain in following Christ far outweighs the losses. You do not know where following Jesus will take you. Neither do you know the specifics of what will be required of you. But you know *who* you are following and can trust Him through every circumstance. You can be fully confident to follow the Lord, no matter where, no matter what, no matter with whom.

If you will commit your life to Christ, you will gain far more than you give up. You will lose your old life, but you will gain a new and abundant life. You will lose this world, but you will gain a far better world to come. You will lose the passing pleasures of sin, but you will gain far better joys in Christ. The positives far outweigh the negatives.

This open invitation to follow Christ is extended to you. But before you answer this invitation, count the cost.

Unconditional Surrender

Or what king, when he sets out to
meet another king in battle, will not
first sit down and consider whether
he is strong enough with ten thousand
men to encounter the one coming
against him with twenty thousand? Or
else, while the other is still far away,
he sends a delegation and asks for
terms of peace (Luke 14:31-32).

The decision to follow Jesus Christ requires the unconditional surrender of our lives to Him. If we are to be His disciples, we must submit to the authority as supreme over us. We must recognize His right to rule our lives and seek to please Him. To come after Him requires that we come to the end of ourselves and relinquish the control of our lives to Him. We must give up all personal rights to the governing power of Christ. This is what is necessary to follow Him.

In the crowd that day, there were those who were uninformed about the high price of following Christ. They were swept up in the excitement of the moment. They had no idea of the demands of Christ, which required that they yield their lives to His lordship. Moreover, they were clueless as to the dangerous condition in which they found themselves. Unknown to them, they were at war with this One whom they were following. Even more serious than this, they were unaware that Christ was at war with them.

In this next parable, Jesus addressed these hard-hitting truths. The One who is 'the truth' (John 14:6) perfectly illustrated the consequences of failing to follow Him on His terms. He told this story involving a military conflict between two adversarial kings. Each monarch has two marching armies at his command. These two rulers are in a state of war with each other. But the confrontation is a terrible mismatch, as the approaching king leads vastly superior soldiers into this conflict. His vastly superior military strength will result in the sure defeat of the lesser king. This outmanned ruler must surrender to the advancing king before it is too late. As we examine this parable, the application for our lives will be obvious.

When Two Kings War

Jesus began by setting the scene: 'Or what king, when he sets out to meet another king in battle' (v. 31). Here, He spoke of these two kings who are at war with each other. Each monarch reigned over his own kingdom. These two sovereigns were entering into battle with each other, lead-ing their respective forces. There was a bitter opposition that existed between them, and a building strife had escalated to a breaking point. They are two powers in intense conflict involving each of their kingdoms. This rivalry was so intense that an incvitable battle was soon to occur.

In this heated clash, only one king will be victorious. These are not two equal powers. One ruler is far superior to the other. The stronger sovereign will easily gain the domination over his weaker foe and will in turn gain the spoils of victory. The lesser king will lose everything and become the slave of the other. The one who suffers defeat will even lose his life. This is a winner-takes-all battle.

The Necessary Calculation

In this parable, Jesus further explains that when the inferior king realizes that he is being threatened by the superior monarch, he must 'first sit down and consider whether he is strong enough with ten thousand men to encounter the one coming against him with twenty thousand' (v. 31). This endangered king must consider what it will mean for him to enter into battle with this dominant despot. He must calculate whether his forces can withstand such an attack. He must weigh his chances against these advancing forces. The under-sized ruler must determine whether he is strong enough with half the soldiers to withstand the assault of this greater king.

The only rational conclusion is this: there is no way that the outnumbered king can prevail against the threat posed by the greater monarch. If he enters into this conflict, he will surely be defeated and destroyed. There is no possibility that the outmanned ruler can stand up to the ruthless aggression of the greater ruler. This short-handed king must come to his senses and soberly realize he is at a severe disadvantage. He must act immediately before it is too late.

The Confronted King

To properly understand this parable, these two powers need to be identified. As Jesus told this story, both of these warring monarchs were standing there that day. The lesser king represented each unconverted person in the crowd that day. By this analogy, each person – much like a king – has the responsibility to preside over the affairs of his kingdom. An enthroned ruler reigns over the business of his domain. A ruler must think carefully about the issues confronting him. His decisions will affect the future of his kingdom.

So it was with each uncommitted person in the crowd. These uncommitted followers were much like a king who ruled over a kingdom. In this case, they presided over the affairs of their own life. The issue of following Christ necessitated their careful deliberation, much like a king when presented with a crisis. What they decide concerning Jesus will not only affect their present conditions, but, ultimately, will determine their eternal destiny. No decision will ever compare with the importance of this one before them.

The Approaching King

In this parable, the other king is the one who is telling this story. This approaching monarch is Jesus Christ Himself, who possesses infinitely greater power. He is the Almighty, the King of kings and Lord of lords (Rev. 19:16). He possesses and exercises absolute sovereignty over every living person. His authority is unrivaled and no foe can withstand

His advances. He claims: 'All authority has been given to Me in heaven and on earth' (Matt. 28:18). Unrivaled authority belongs to Him alone.

Concerning this King, the Bible says: 'And to Him was given dominion, glory and a kingdom, that all the peoples, nations and men of every language might serve Him. His dominion is an everlasting dominion which will not pass away; And His kingdom is one which will not be destroyed' (Dan. 7:14). Paul maintained that God the Father 'raised [Christ] from the dead and seated Him at His right hand in the heavenly *places*, far above all rule and authority and power and dominion, and every name that is named, not only in this age but also in the one to come. And He put all things in subjection under His feet' (Eph. 1:20-22). This statement announces the unlimited sovereignty of Jesus Christ over all the universe and this includes every single person on earth.

Every human life is subjected beneath the omnipotence of Jesus Christ. Every person is subordinate to His decisions. Paul wrote: 'God highly exalted Him, and bestowed on Him the name which is above every name, so that at the name of Jesus EVERY KNEE WILL BOW, of those who are in heaven and on earth and under the earth, and that every tongue will confess that Jesus Christ is Lord, to the glory of God the Father' (Phil. 2:9-11). This statement reveals His exalted position over all heaven and earth.

The Conflict of the Ages

This parable teaches the hostile war that exists between sinful man and holy God. They are not at peace with each other, but are, in fact, in severe conflict. The lesser king is at war with the greater king. This represents the spiritual enmity that every unconverted person has for Jesus Christ. Those in the crowd that day did not realize the state of war in which they found themselves. But it is their unbelief that has put them into this spiritual warfare against God. They were not in peacetime conditions with Him, but in a state of declared war.

The rest of the Bible confirms this truth. Every unbeliever finds himself in cosmic rebellion against heaven's King. Jesus said: 'He who is not with Me is against Me' (Matt. 12:30). Paul states that all unbelievers are 'enemies' of God (Rom. 5:10). Moreover, they are 'alienated and hostile in mind, engaged in evil deeds' (Col. 1:21). This is the spiritual treason of the human race against almighty God.

Warring Christ

This parable, however, teaches something even more sobering. It pictures Jesus Christ at war with sinners who refuse to repent and surrender to Him. In speaking 'the wrath to come,' John the Baptist warned that irreversible judgment was imminent: 'The axe is already laid at the root of the trees; therefore every tree that does not bear fruit is cut down and thrown into the fire' (Matt. 3:10). Jesus Christ Himself will be the Executer of this divine wrath against all unbelievers.

Jesus is the One who 'judges and wages war' (Rev. 19:11). Scripture says: 'And the armies which are in heaven, clothed in fine linen, white *and* clean, were following Him on white horses. From His mouth comes a sharp sword, so that with it He may strike down the nations, and He will rule them with a rod of iron; and He treads the wine press of the fierce wrath of God, the Almighty' (Rev. 19:14-15).

The application was unmistakable. Jesus issued this warning to those in the crowd who were not in a neutral state with Him. There is no neutral state with Christ. We are either on His side or at war with Him. And yet He offers peace through His terms to all His enemies, but they must accept them in full. He extended grace to them in this invitation, but they must respond with their surrender because He is approaching in the final judgment. This is a hard truth, but truth nonetheless.

Terms of Peace

As this parable concludes, Jesus explained the mercy He offered to the crowd. It was found in the form of this superior king who offered terms of peace: 'Or else, while the other is still far away he sends a delegation and asks for terms of peace' (v. 32). The encroaching king with vastly superior forces offers the possibility of reconciliation. The only rational decision for the inferior king to make was to surrender. If the outmanned king does not accept this truce, he will lose the battle. Any sane ruler would come to his senses and accept his offer of peace. This lesser king cannot withstand this greater king. This superior king is coming but offers to end the war with his terms of peace.

In this parable, the terms of peace are found in the cross of the Lord Jesus Christ. It is Christ alone who makes peace between God and man. The Bible says: 'Therefore, having been justified by faith, we have peace with God through our Lord Jesus Christ' (Rom. 5:1). This peace is exclusively found in Jesus Christ, who is 'our peace' (Eph. 2:14). In His first coming the apostle Paul states: 'AND HE CAME AND PREACHED PEACE TO YOU WHO WERE FAR AWAY, AND PEACE TO THOSE WHO WERE NEAR' (Eph. 2:17). By His substitutionary death, Jesus 'made peace through the blood of His cross' (Col. 1:20). This is the free offer of 'the gospel of peace' (Eph. 6:15) to those under the wrath of God. The good news is that God in Christ will forgive the offenses of His enemies, no matter how immense.

The Terms of Peace

Jesus Christ extends to you His terms of peace. He will end the warfare between God and you. This is the offer of reconciliation with God. No right-thinking person will want to enter into conflict with Jesus Christ on the final day. You must respond to His invitation that requires your full surrender. You cannot cut your own deal with Him. He will not negotiate. The invitation is to accept His terms of peace.

Jesus is calling for your verdict. Accept His offer before it is too late. You must unconditionally surrender your life to Him.

UNDER NEW MANAGEMENT

So then, none of you can be My
disciple who does not give up all his
own possessions (Luke 14:33).

As Jesus sized up the crowd following Him, He rightly
assessed where they stood in relationship with Him.
With penetrating insight, He saw into their very hearts.
He concluded that they needed to surrender their lives
to Him. Their entire beings yet needed to come under
His authority. Everything they were, everything they
did and everything they had must come under His
control.

This becomes clear in the next statement Jesus made: 'So then, none of you can be My disciple who does not give up all his own possessions' (Luke 14:33). I want us to look carefully at this demanding statement. Once we understand its true meaning, its implications for our lives are staggering.

A Sharp Negative

Jesus began this part of His discourse with a strong negative. This was so that His sharp words would have a cutting edge to them. He maintained: 'None of you can be My disciple.' These blunt words are abrupt. It hardly seems the way to invite others to follow you. But this is exactly how Jesus issued this summons. His biting words were intended to jolt the crowd to do some careful thinking and assessment. He was saying that none of them could be His disciple unless the following condition was met.

By saying 'none of you can be My disciple,' Jesus was indicating that they could not continue going along with Him in an uncommitted manner. They could no longer be merely curious and certainly not cavalier. They must come to the point of personal commitment to Him.

Every disciple, Jesus said, must 'give up all his own possessions' (v. 33). What did our Lord mean by this statement? Is salvation for sale? Must forgiveness of sin be bought? Must we give everything that we own away?

Buying Salvation?

First, Jesus was *not* saying that those in the crowd must purchase their salvation. No amount of material assets can secure a right standing before God. He was not meaning that they must liquidate their material assets in order to buy a ticket to heaven. He was not requiring that they must pay their way into heaven. The entire Bible speaks with one voice in teaching that salvation is a free gift. Grace is offered without cost through the finished work of Jesus Christ upon the cross.

Beginning in the Old Testament, this was abundantly clear. The prophet states: 'Ho! Every one who thirsts, come to the waters; And you who have no money come, buy and eat. Come, buy wine and milk without money and without cost. "Why do you spend money for what is not bread, and your wages for what does not satisfy?"' (Isa. 55:1-2). God is saying that salvation can never be purchased with money. It cannot be bartered for with one's wages. The forgiveness of sins is not up for bid or sale. No amount of money could buy freedom out of the slave market of sin. The debt incurred by sin against God is simply too great to be moved by any human resources.

The apostle Peter confirms this fact when he writes: 'you were not redeemed with perishable things like silver or gold from your futile way of life inherited from your forefathers, but with precious blood, as of a lamb unblemished and spotless, the *blood* of Christ' (1 Pet. 1:18-19). No person has enough gold or silver to purchase any acceptance with God. No amount of money can remove sin in the human soul, grace alone through the cross is the only remedy.

Becoming Paupers?

Second, Jesus is *not* saying that those who would be His disciples must take a vow of poverty. He is not advocating becoming a pauper as the means to salvation or spirituality. Christ is not teaching that His followers must divest themselves of all worldly goods. Such a dispossession would be senseless. If His disciples sold all they owned, then unbelievers would have to feed and clothe them. This would be a miserable witness to a perishing world.

To the contrary, the Bible teaches that if a man does not care for the members of his own household, he is worse than an infidel (1 Tim. 5:8). This clearly implies that the head of the house has financial resources at his disposal. He must use them to care for his family. This indicates that the husband is a hard worker and a breadwinner. He acquires wealth. The money he earns is to be used to feed and clothe his own family. It would be shameful if someone else had to provide for his own family because he gave away all his money.

Moreover, Christians have a moral responsibility to help a fellow believer who is in physical need. They are expected to have riches and use them to meet the needs of others: 'If a brother or sister is without clothing and in need of daily food, and one of you says to them, "Go in peace, be warmed and be filled," and yet you do not give them what is necessary for *their* body, what use is that' (James 2:15-16)? Again we read: 'But whoever has the world's goods, and sees his brother in need and closes his heart against him, how does the love of God abide in him' (1 John 3:17)? If a disciple fails to provide for the needs of another disciple, it calls into question his love for God.

Furthermore, Jesus told several parables that were based upon the banking industry. Here, Christ commended possession, lending, and borrowing of money. The shrewd investing of resources is a virtue, not a vice. The apostle Paul adds that the love of money, not the possession of it, is the root of all evil (1 Tim. 6:10). Some of the most notable believers in the Bible were rich by the standards of their day. Such financially well-endowed men included Abraham, Job, Solomon, and Joseph of Arimathea.

Let us be clear, Jesus was not teaching that His followers must give away all their assets before they can enter into His kingdom. And we see that neither was He implying that one must buy the grace that only God gives. So what did Jesus mean?

Stewards, Not Owners

Instead, what Christ is teaching in this statement – 'must give up all his own possessions' – is this: every disciple must recognize that they have come under His lordship. In other words, they have come under new management. As His follower, he realizes that he is merely a steward of what Christ has placed into his hands. A steward is a house manager, meaning one who oversees the possessions of his master. However, he himself owns nothing. He manages the properties that belong to the head of the house. A steward merely acts on behalf of his master in handling his assets. He lives in his master's house and oversees his belongings. He uses them to conduct his lord's business. But he himself ultimately owns nothing.

This is the point Jesus was making with the crowd. They must see themselves as stewards of what they have. Their money will remain in their own pocket. But it must now be recognized as ultimately belonging to God. They will no longer be the owner of what they have, but merely the trustee. Those who follow Christ become a manager of what has been entrusted to them. Earthly things must now be wisely used for the greater glory of God. Earthly treasures can no longer be used for selfish purposes. They must be invested in what will further the work of the kingdom.

Let me make this personal. If you are to become a disciple of Christ, your entire life will no longer be your life. Your whole life will belong to Him. Your time will no longer be your time. Instead, it will be His time to be used for His purposes. Your talents will no longer be your talents. Rather, they will become His and used for His purposes. Your treasure will no longer be your treasure, but simply entrusted to you for this brief time of your life. You must recognize that all that you are and have must be seen as ultimately His. In this sense, you come under new management.

A Forbidden Love

A disciple must no longer love most the things of this world. He must supremely love God. The Bible warns: 'Do not love the world nor the things in the world. If anyone loves the world, the love of the Father is not in him. For all that is in the world, the lust of the flesh and the lust of the eyes and the boastful pride of life, is not from the Father, but is from the world' (1 John 2:15-16). A disciple may use the things of this world, and even enjoy these things. But they must never capture and control his affections. Chief passions are reserved exclusively for God.

This is precisely what Jesus meant: 'Do not store up for yourselves treasures on earth, where moth and rust destroy, and where thieves break in and steal. But store up for yourselves treasures in heaven, where neither moth nor rust destroys, and where thieves do not break in or steal; for where your treasure is, there your heart will be also (Matt. 6:19-21). A disciple does not live to accumulate possessions in this life. He invests what he has in eternal purposes. Jesus continued: 'No one can serve two masters; for either he will hate the one and love the other, or he will be devoted to one and despise the other. You cannot serve God and wealth' (Matt. 6:24). The Lord did not condemn the possession of wealth, but denounced serving money and putting your trust and security ultimately in it.

Obtaining Eternal Life

Jesus was once approached by a rich young ruler, who asked: 'Teacher, what good thing shall I do that I may obtain eternal life?' (Matt. 19:16). By this question, this successful individual expressed that he wanted to gain salvation. Yet at the same time, he wanted to live for the things in this world. He wanted to add Jesus to his life, while still living for this world.

Jesus responded: 'Why are you asking Me about what is good? There is only One who is good' (v. 17). This prosperous person was ignorant of whom he was addressing. Jesus was clarifying that He was more than a teacher. He was God in human flesh—truly God and truly man.

Keeping the Law

This young man failed to see the perfect holiness of Jesus. Therefore, he failed to see his own unholiness. So, Jesus used the Law to reveal this man's sin. He said to him: 'if you wish to enter into life, keep the commandments' (v. 17). Jesus was not saying that this young man could earn salvation through perfect obedience. Quite the opposite, he was showing that he actually could not do so.

This high-end over-achiever responded: 'Then he said to Him, "Which ones?" And Jesus responded, "YOU SHALL NOT COMMIT MURDER; YOU SHALL NOT COMMIT ADULTERY; YOU SHALL NOT STEAL; YOU SHALL NOT BEAR FALSE WITNESS; HONOR YOUR FATHER AND MOTHER; and YOU SHALL LOVE YOUR NEIGHBOR AS YOURSELF" ' (vv. 18-19). With these five commandments, Jesus gave this man the second tablet of the Law. This was the easier part of the commandments to keep. The young man confidently replied: 'All these things I have kept; what am I still lacking?' (v. 20). He was naively oblivious to his own sin.

Loving Money

In this encounter, Jesus saw into his heart and detected his all-consuming love of possessions. Jesus needed to dig deeper and expose his sin of covetousness. Christ saw that money was his main passion. He said: 'If you wish to be complete, go *and* sell your possessions and give to *the* poor, and you will have treasure in heaven; and come, follow Me' (Matt. 19:21). Jesus was not saying that he could not possess money. Rather, He meant, money could not possess him.

This cost was too high for this rich man. 'But when the young man heard this statement, he went away grieving; for he was one who owned much property' (v. 22). This young ruler turned and walked away from Christ. He loved his earthly riches more than a spiritual inheritance. He refused to abandon his old master—money—in order to receive a new Master—Jesus Christ.

Making the Point

This is precisely the point that Jesus was making with these large crowds. If any of them were to become His disciple, they must come under new management. They must give Him the place of supreme love and loyalty in their lives. They must hold everything they have with an open hand with Him. He must become their number one priority. They must love Christ more than the things in this world.

This is, likewise, what Jesus is saying to you. Christ offers salvation to you as a free gift. It must be received by faith alone. But true faith involves the complete surrender of your life to Christ. Saving faith is entrusting your entire being to Him.

Where Are You?

Have you come to this place? Do you see that it is not a reward to be earned? Instead, the grace of God is a free gift offered to you. Have you received this gift?

Following Jesus requires far more than merely being in a religious crowd. Being a disciple is an internal, personal reality. Coming to Christ requires surrendering your life to Him and such a commitment encompasses every area of your life. Everything you are and everything you possess must be seen by this reality. In short, you must come under His new management.

Have you taken this decisive step of faith? If you come to Jesus with childlike faith, He will receive you.

Tasteless Salt

Therefore, salt is good; but if even
salt has become tasteless, with what
will it be seasoned? It is useless either
for the soil or for the manure pile; it
is thrown out (Luke 14:34-35a).

Those in the crowd following Jesus must have been won-
dering when He would lighten the message. This has been
a hard-hitting address. They must have expected that Jesus
would balance His message at some point by softening it.
They must have anticipated that Jesus would eventually
lighten His demands. Will He lower the admission requirements to enter the kingdom? Will He not meet them half-
way?

The answer is no. Rather than lessening His demands, Jesus maintained the provocative challenge of His words. Being a follower of Christ is far too important for a shallow presentation. The critical nature of this subject concerns the eternal destiny of their souls. Due to the significance of the message, however, Jesus continued to speak the sobering words of true discipleship. The full weight of what He had to say struck hard in the hearts of the crowd. His teaching was straightforward. His truth was arresting. His demands were non-negotiable. These words by Jesus hit them with the force of a category five hurricane. It was not hard to understand, just hard to swallow.

What Christ will say next has major implications for every one of us. This message cannot be dismissed as being reserved for this first century crowd. This truth cannot be avoided by relegating it to ancient times. Rather, these words are as relevant today as when they were first spoken. They apply as directly to you and me as when Jesus first uttered them. So, we must give our careful consideration to what they require of us.

A Positive Commodity

In this next verse, Jesus brought what He had been saying to them to a dramatic conclusion. He introduced these words by stating another general truth from everyday life. He began: 'Therefore, salt is good' (v. 34). Everyone could understand this. All could agree with this. Salt is good because it is useful for human life. Salt preserves meat from spoiling. Salt imparts flavor to otherwise bland food. Salt cleanses what is unclean. Salt even possesses medical properties that heal an open wound.

A disciple, Jesus said, is likened to salt. He had made this comparison earlier in the Sermon on the Mount when He said to His disciples: 'You are the salt of the earth' (Matt. 5:13). All followers of Christ are the salt of the earth. By their presence in society, they were to bring a moral influence upon the world. They were to retard the sinful corruption of the world. The penetrating impact of their personal holiness was to be a preventative force in their surroundings. Disciples were not to be the sugar of the earth. But like salt, they were to sting the raw wounds of the world's immorality, producing a cleansing effect upon those around them. Each of these sanctifying aspects was to be produced in the lives of those following Christ.

Salt That Loses Its Savor

However, Jesus followed His initial statement with a stern warning: 'but even if salt has become tasteless, with what will it be seasoned?' (v. 34). Jesus was indicating that not all salt is genuine. Some salt initially appears to be real but then in reality, it is not. Some background is necessary. In this part of the world, there was a salty, rock-like mineral that had gypsum mixed with it. This hybrid rock – half salt and half gypsum – was not real salt. It was an easy-to-mistake imitation. Upon closer scrutiny, this alternate stone would eventually show itself to be a counterfeit substitute for salt. This mineral looked like the real thing but when sampled, it did not taste like authentic salt. This is because though it appeared to be salt, it was not genuine.

By this metaphor, the Lord was making a critical point. He was contrasting a true disciple and a false one. The latter kind of follower merely had an outward façade of being a genuine disciple. But in reality he was not. He gave the outward appearance of being an authentic disciple. But internally, he was devoid of the authenticity of a true follower of Christ.

Tasteless salt, Jesus said, had no use. Neither did uncommitted disciples. Those in the crowd with a divided heart were like this fake salt. They were not committed to Christ. Consequently, they possessed no moral influence. They were worthless to hold back the corrupting influence of evil in the world. They did not add any zest and flavor to the lives of others. They are like salt that had become tasteless. Though giving the outward appearance of being a true disciple, they in reality, were not. Their superficial commitment betrayed a wholehearted loyalty to Christ.

Can It Be Restored?

Jesus then asked this rhetorical question concerning tasteless salt: 'With what will it be seasoned?' This was a pressing inquiry that implied a negative answer. The answer is so obvious that Jesus did not bother to answer it. This kind of phony salt is good for nothing. Earlier in His ministry, Jesus asserted: 'If the salt has become tasteless, how can it be made salty again?' (Matt. 5:13). The same negative answer is assumed. Real salt cannot become unsalty. Neither can tasteless salt become true salt.

Many in the crowd appeared to be salt. But these were not genuinely converted to Him. They only had a thin veneer of religiosity. They looked spiritual while mixed in with this religious crowd. But, when with a different crowd, their true nature would be revealed. When with a different throng, they are easily squeezed into the mold of the world. They were not in danger of losing their salvation. They could not lose what they did not already possess. The truth is, they had never been converted to Christ. In due time, their true spiritual colors will be revealed. This is what Jesus is teaching in this text. Those in the crowd would soon lose their saltiness and it is revealed that they were never genuine salt.

Good for Nothing

Jesus followed this statement with biting sarcasm: 'It is useless either for the soul or for the manure pile' (v. 35). He was asserting that tasteless salt is good for nothing. Imitation salt is not even good to be thrown into the manure pile. In this day, they did not have the modern convenience of indoor plumbing. Consequently, human waste was collected in a clay pot. It was carried outside the house to be thrown onto a dung pile. The stench was offensive to anyone's sensibilities. To retard the foul smell, salt was thrown onto the excrement. However, what only looks like salt has in actuality no capacity to curb this loathsome odor. Such fake salt was entirely useless to perform even this base function. This is how Jesus described the half-committed crowd. They were entirely useless to God and His purposes.

Those not fully devoted to Jesus were like counterfeit salt that had lost its flavor. Such members of the multitude had zero benefit to the kingdom of God. Such a marginal person made no positive contribution to the mission of Jesus Christ. This kind of person – half in, half out with Christ – had no eternal value for the purposes of God.

Such a crowd-follower was not a Christ-follower. This person had no decisive commitment to Jesus Christ. He had only a superficial attachment to Christ. This person had not yet come to know Jesus personally.

A Call for Self-Examination

These words by Jesus Christ are a serious call for self-examination. An unexamined life is a dangerous life to live. Such a superficial life is the breeding ground for self-deception. This was true with the twelve disciples, even among those the closest to the Lord Jesus, one of them was tasteless salt. His name was Judas. He was a false disciple. Though he had a close association to Jesus, he had no saving relationship with Him. He was religious, yet lost. There were Judases in this religious crowd going along with Jesus. In the same way, many in the religious crowd today are not genuine followers of Christ.

The apostle Paul writes: 'Test yourselves to see if you are in the faith; examine yourselves!' (2 Cor. 13:5). Everyone who hears the word of God should audit their own soul. They should ask themselves: am I genuinely converted to Christ? Do I see the evidence of a changed life? Have I sincerely called upon the name of the Lord for salvation? Do I have a living relationship with Jesus Christ?

Untold multitudes profess faith in Jesus, but do not truly know Him. Many are in church, but are not in Christ. Many are religious, but not regenerated.

Could this be true of you? Could you be clinging to an empty conversion experience that was not genuine? Could you lack the assurance of your salvation because you do not possess it?

If there is any doubt about where you are with the Lord, I hope you are hearing the words of Jesus here. The Bible also says: 'Seek the Lord while He may be found; Call upon Him while He is near' (Isa. 55:6). This is the time for you to seek the Lord. He is near to you. There is saving grace waiting for you in Him. And He will receive you.

EARS TO HEAR

He who has ears to hear, let him hear
(Luke 14:35).

Those in the crowd following Jesus heard what He said.
His words were nothing less than powerful and penetrating.
What He said was stunning and shocking. The teaching of
Christ was unmistakably clear. They had never heard any-
thing like this. No man ever spoke as He did.

But strangely enough, many in this crowd did not hear
what Jesus said. Sure, they heard His audible speech. Their
physical ears took in the sound of what He said. But few

actually heard the reality and truth of what He said. Most who heard Him did not actually hear Him. Not all heard Him with spiritual ears to hear the truth. The challenging words Jesus spoke were only received by a small number within this larger crowd.

To reach their hearts, Jesus issued a final challenge. It is as if He grabbed them by their shoulders and shook them to get their attention. So, Jesus concluded with these words: 'He who has ears to hear, let him hear' (v. 35). What did He mean by this? Did not everyone have two ears with which to hear Him? Why would Jesus say this? Of course, they heard Him. Or did they?

Spiritual Ears Needed

This urgent plea by the Lord Jesus called upon the crowd to listen with spiritual ears. He urged them to give their utmost attention to what He had said. Granted, they heard the truth with their natural ears, but they needed to receive what He said with spiritual ears. For these words to proceed from their heads into their hearts, they would need spiritual ears. Only then could His words be internalized into their hearts and souls. Then they had the responsibility to rightly respond. For to hear but not to do, was not to hear at all.

Tragically, many in the crowd that day did not hear what He was saying. For different reasons, many—if not most—in the crowd had turned spiritually deaf ears to His demands. A few heard Him with discerning ears, but only a small percentage of the crowd. Why did so many truly not hear the words of Jesus? Why did they have ears, but not hear? If this crowd was like most assemblies, a variety of reasons prevented them from hearing what Jesus was truly saying.

Mental Distractions

First, some in the crowd did not hear Jesus because they would have been mentally preoccupied with other matters. They were physically present with Christ. But they were mentally absent. Their bodies were there, but their minds were somewhere else. Many in the crowd would have been easily distracted with other concerns. Their minds would have been drifting onto various temporal matters in their lives. They could have been distracted by matters back at home, or with work, or family or even with who was there that day.

Jesus said that when the word goes forth, this would be one of the responses. In the parable of the sower, He explained that many 'hear,' but 'did not hear' (Matt. 13:17). One reason was because when the seed of the word was sown into hearts, it fell 'among the thorns,' 'the worry of the world' choked it (Matt. 13:22). Such concerns with the things of this world prevent many from hearing what Jesus said.

Many today are similarly distracted when the gospel is made known. They sit in church under the sound of the word. But their mind is far away. Their thoughts are elsewhere. The word goes in one ear and out the other. They hear, but do not really hear. They daydream under the preaching of the gospel. Is your mind wandering elsewhere as this is being presented to you? This truth requires you give strictest attention to what Jesus has said.

Everyone who hears the word is commanded to be 'quick to hear, slow to speak and slow to anger' (James 1:19). You must strive to be a careful listener when the word is proclaimed and seek to understand what the Lord is truly saying. When the word is spoken, Jesus is speaking and you must be listening. Be slow to argue with His teaching, for excuses will only dull our hearing. Pay keen attention to what you hear from the lips of our Lord, for therein is life and salvation.

Physical Limitations

Second, others in the crowd would have been growing physically tired and weak. Most would have gone without food and water for some period of time. That had been the case earlier when Jesus fed the five thousand men plus untold numbers of women and children (John 6:1-14). Food and water were hard to come by in the first century with such a large crowd. Increasing hunger and thirst would have been a barrier to hearing Jesus' teaching. Their feet would have been sore from the walking. Their backs would have been aching from standing. Their faces would have been scorched from the glaring hot sun. Their lips would have been parched. These conditions would have made it hard to be attentive to the word Jesus was preaching that day.

So it is with many today. They do not actually hear the word of God because they are limited by physical limitations. They have stayed up late on Saturday night, then they come dragging into church on Sunday morning. They are late for the service. They have had little or no breakfast. They have no energy to listen to the word being preached. They daydream during the sermon. They zone out of the message. They doze off while the word is preached. Is it any wonder that they do not receive what they hear?

Emotional Hysterias

Third, still others would have been unable to hear what Jesus said because they were too emotionally drained. The excitement of the crowd would have whipped them up into a euphoric high. They would have become incapable of exercising the rational thought needed to hear the message. Their hearts would have outrun their heads. There was undoubtedly a crowd dynamic that would have caused people to be swept up in the adrenaline rush of the moment.

Many in the crowd would have been caught up in the hysteria of looking for the supernatural display of His power. They had heard how He healed the sick. They knew about how He cast out demons. They even heard the reports that He had raised the dead. But this preoccupation with the physical would have curbed appetite for the spiritual. On one occasion, Jesus withdrew from the people because they wanted to see miracles. He responded, 'Let us go somewhere else to the towns nearby, so that I may preach there also; for that is what I came for' (Mark 1:38). The spiritual priority that Jesus placed upon His earthly ministry was preaching the word, not performing miracles.

In like manner, there are many people today who do not hear what Jesus teaches in His word because of their obsession with miracles. They are easily led astray because they want to see a display of the supernatural before their eyes. But this is why they do not hear with their ears. It is their fixation with miracles that makes them completely miss the message.

Such a state of hyper-excitement would have prevented people from hearing the words of Christ. His teaching about their own spiritual condition would have been muted.

As a result, they would have failed to hear what Jesus was saying due to this focus on their emotions and experience.

Could this rush of excitement hold you back from hearing the word? Maybe you attend a church where frenzied emotions outrace the depth of intellect. Could it be that the straightforward truth of the Scripture is being crowded out by the revved up emotional highs? If so, you could be easily prevented from hearing the real truth that Jesus is speaking to you. It is crucial to give careful thought to what the Lord is saying in His word. Do you hear the spiritual truth He taught?

Spiritual Indifference

Fourth, others in this crowd would have been spiritually indifferent toward what He was saying. Their overexposure to the truth would have caused them to be apathetic to it. A vaccine gives a small dose of the disease that prevents someone from contracting the real thing. In like manner, an abundant exposure to the gospel without responding to it would have caused some to be further unresponsive to it. In such a scenario, their heads were full of the truth. But it never penetrated into their hearts. It remained mere head knowledge that had never effected their affections. As a result, the truth never moved their wills to truly believe.

Such people could have easily recited what Jesus preached. They could give an accurate restatement of His words. They knew the nuances of the doctrine that He had taught and could give a cogent summary of what He had expounded. They could even articulate it back to others. But the message Jesus gave never truly penetrated their hearts.

The truth had never opened up their inner soul and revealed their sin. They saw no need for His grace in salvation.

It had never brought conviction of sin. The teaching of Christ had never caused them to seek God with all their being and, thus, the invitation of Christ had never been answered by a surrendered will.

Maybe that is where you are. Perhaps you are well taught in the teaching of Christ and even have a head full of sound doctrine. You can give an adequate explanation of the Christian faith. You have a Bible and other spiritual books, and yet an empty life. Maybe you are even involved in teaching the truth to others. But could it be that this truth has not gone deeper in your life? Has it ever progressed beyond your mind and into your heart? If this describes you, ask God to bring the truth home to your heart. Ask Him to give you ears to hear. Ask Him to take it from your head to your very heart and soul.

Personal Deception

Fifth, still others in the multitude would have heard what Jesus said, but wrongly assumed the message was for others, and not for them. Many deceived themselves into presuming that they were right with God, but in reality this was far from the case. Because they were a part of this religious crowd, they believed they must be in the kingdom of God as well. They had this close proximity to Jesus and were even walking along with Him. By hearing the words of Christ, they came to assume that they also believed the message.

But nothing could have been farther from the truth. They had proximity to Christ, but did not possess Him. They walked alongside Jesus, but did not follow Him. They beheld Him, but did not believe in Him. They heard Him, but did not heed Him.

Untold numbers today are self-deceived just like they were. Countless church members perceive that because they attend church, they must be acceptable to God. Tragically, they have an empty hope of a salvation that they do not actually and personally possess. The reason they assume they are a child of God is due to their association with other believers. The sad reality is, such individuals have professed Christ, but have never come all the way to Christ. They have assumed a relationship with Christ based upon their own terms. Truth be known, they have never denied themselves, taken up a cross, and followed Christ.

Where Are You?

'What is the condition of your heart? Are you alive in Christ? Have you believed in Him alone for your salvation? Have you been given spiritual ears to hear this great message? To truly hear and understand the gospel you must have this spiritual hearing from above. It must go from your head to your heart resulting in true belief and commitment to Christ. You must see your need for Him and admit your only hope is found in Him.

Seek Him today while He may be found. Ask Him to open your deaf ears and give you the faith to believe these words. Is there something holding you back from coming all the way to Him? Have you admitted your need and reliance on Him alone, forsaking everything else? Will you take this decisive step of faith and come to Christ? He stands ready to save you even today.

13

LASTING WORDS

He who has ears to hear, let him hear
(Luke 14:35).

Last words should be lasting words. What someone says last often has a lingering effect upon us. So it should be with these words of Christ. This last chapter should really capture our attention due to its placement and importance. Last words should last.

Here is what should resonate in your heart. The words of Jesus Christ are addressed to your total person. This includes your mind, emotions, and will. The gospel wants to instruct your mind. It wants to ignite your affections. And it wants to influence your will. In this closing chapter, I want to leave you with this effect.

What You Must *Know*

First, if you are to make a commitment to Jesus Christ, you need to *know* the truth. The gospel teaches that the Lord Jesus Christ is the eternal Son of God who became the Son of Man. He was sent by God the Father into this world to rescue lost sinners from eternal destruction under His righteous anger. Jesus was born of a woman and entered the human race and yet was born of a virgin in order to be without sin. He was truly God and truly man.

You must *know* the sinless life of Jesus. He was born under the Law in order to obey the commands that you have repeatedly broken. He alone achieved perfect righteousness that is credited to the account of all who believe in Him. Through this, God sees all believers as though they have kept the Law with full obedience.

You must *know* the sin-bearing death of Jesus. Being sinless, He was qualified to die in the place of guilty sinners. He was lifted up on the cruel cross in order to become sin for all who would believe in Him. Upon the blood-stained cross, Jesus bore our sins and secured the salvation of sinners. He is the only way of salvation. Jesus said: 'I am the way, and the truth, and the life; no one comes to the Father but through Me' (John 14:6). Jesus alone leads to heaven; there is no other alternative. The Bible says: 'There is salvation in no one else; for there is no other name under heaven that has been given among men by which we must be saved' (Acts 4:12).

You must *know* the bodily resurrection of Jesus. He was buried in a borrowed tomb. On the third day, He raised Himself from the dead. This resurrection was the vindication by God that His death was a fully sufficient sacrifice to take away the sins of all believers. He then ascended back to the right hand of God the Father. He is now enthroned on high, possessing all authority in heaven and earth. The Bible declares: 'WHOEVER SHALL CALL UPON THE NAME OF THE LORD WILL BE SAVED' (Rom. 10:13).

You must also *know* the gospel invitation of Jesus. As Jesus called to the crowd two thousand years ago, He is calling you to come to Him. He pleads: 'Come to Me, all who are weary and heavy-laden, and I will give you rest. Take My yoke upon you and learn from Me, for I am gentle and humble in heart, and YOU WILL FIND REST FOR YOUR SOULS. For My yoke is easy and My burden is light' (Matt. 11:28-30). You must respond to this invitation He issues. It is an invitation we can only respond to by a step of faith and by the Holy Spirit drawing you. This is what you must *know*.

What You Must *Feel*

Second, if you are to become a follower of Christ, there is something you must *feel*: You must feel your need of Him. You must feel the weight of your sin upon you and your lostness without Jesus Christ. Without the bad news, there is no good news. This is how God designed the gospel, and this truth is not optional. You must feel this is order to be a genuine disciple of Jesus Christ.

You must *feel* the conviction of the Holy Spirit. The Spirit has come into the world to convict you of your need of Christ. Jesus said, that the Spirit 'will convict the world concerning sin and righteousness and judgment; concerning sin, because they do not believe in Me; and concerning righteousness, because I go to the Father and you no longer see Me; and concerning judgment, because the ruler of this world has been judged' (John 16:8-11). This work of the Spirit is to convince you of your need for Christ in the gospel. The Spirit must press this truth so strongly to your heart that you feel the desperate longing for Him.

You must *feel* your unbelief. The Holy Spirit will convict us of 'sin,' Jesus said, 'because they do not believe in Me' (John 16:9). The violation of God's word will damn anyone's soul if they do not trust in Jesus Christ for payment of their sin instead. The Spirit convinces unbelievers of their unbelief in Jesus. Every sin can be forgiven except this ultimate sin. To die in this sin is to commit 'blasphemy against the Holy Spirit' (Matt. 12:31). The greatest sin is actually the failure to believe in Jesus Christ.

You must *feel* your lack of righteousness. The Holy Spirit has also come to convict the world of 'righteousness,' Jesus added: 'because I go to My Father and you no longer see Me' (John 16:10). This statement means that Jesus will judge the world in absolute righteousness (Acts 17:31). All who die in unbelief regarding Jesus will then be judged by Him. 'Books' will also be opened, which contain every sin a person has committed in their life (Rev. 20:12). 'The book of life' will be opened, and it will reveal that their names were never recorded in it. Every person without faith in Christ will be rightly and justly judged in perfect righteousness by Christ. Every sin will receive a 'just penalty' (Heb. 2:2).

You must *feel* the gravity of the final judgment. Moreover, the Holy Spirit will also convict the world of 'judgment, because the ruler of this world has been judged.' Christ's victory over Satan anticipates His judgment of all sinners. No one will escape the final judgment by Christ, all must stand before Him. In an argument from the greater to the lesser, if the ruler of this world has been judged, how much more will his lesser subjects who served him in the kingdom of darkness. This last judgment is rendered by Jesus Christ into whose hands all judgment has been assigned by the Father (John 5:22). If the devil has been judged, so also will all his children of darkness.

Do you feel this hopelessness of your condition before God without faith in Christ? Do you feel how unclean you are before the Lord? This is what we must all feel when measured next to God's perfect holiness and is the correct response to this judgment.

What You Must *Do*

Third, if you are to follow Christ, there is also something you must *do*. It is not enough to know these truths of the gospel. Nor is it enough to feel your need for Jesus Christ. You must go one step further. As an act of your will, you must believe upon Jesus Christ. You must repent and believe the gospel. Jesus announced to His generation, 'Repent and believe in the gospel' (Mark 1:15). The word repentance means a change of mind that produces a change of heart and will. This leads inevitably to a change of life.

You must have a change of mind. Repentance requires that you have a change of thinking about God, Christ, and yourself. You must see God as an infinitely holy God who requires moral perfection in order to enter His presence. You must see yourself as a sinner who has fallen short of the glory of His holiness and thus deserving of eternal punishment. You need to agree with His judgment of your life and finally turn to the Lord Jesus Christ and trust Him wholly.

You must then have a change of direction. Repentance also requires that you turn away from your sin, including your own efforts to save yourself. Then in faith, turn to Jesus Christ, who alone is the Savior of the world. This turning involves a decisive about face. It requires a complete reversal. There must be a pivot away from the world and sin. There must be a turning to Jesus Christ alone.

You must have a change of will. This is taking an active step of faith to commit your life to Jesus Christ. Faith forsakes all else and trusts Him alone for the forgiveness of sin and the obtaining of His righteousness. Faith looks to Christ. Faith trusts Christ. Faith submits to Him. Faith loves Him. Faith receives Him. Without faith, we cannot have Christ. Thankfully, our faith originates within God and He then bestows to us in salvation.

Will you believe in Him? Will you trust Him? Will you acknowledge His right to rule over your life? Will you deny yourself, take up a cross, and follow Him?

Take That Step of Faith

Have you done this? Have you committed your life to Jesus Christ? Have you turned away from your life pursuit of sin? Have you entrusted your life to His saving hands? Have you surrendered to Him who died upon the cross for you?

This very moment, the gates of Paradise are swung wide open to you. You may come through the narrow gate now. The Lord Jesus will receive you to Himself. He says that 'whoever comes to Me I will never cast out' (John 6:37). He is calling to you right now. He is inviting you to come to Him this very moment. Take that final step of faith and come all the way to Him.

If you will become a true follower of Christ, you will have the heavy weight of your sin lifted off you. You will have the yoke of Christ placed upon you. Jesus Christ gets into the yoke with you and pulls with you.

I Am A Disciple

I close with this piece that I came across several years ago. It is entitled *I Am a Disciple*.

The die has been cast.
I have stepped over the line.
The decision has been made.
I am a disciple of Jesus Christ.

I will not look up,
    let up,
    slow down,
    back away,
    or be still.
I no longer need preeminence,
    prosperity,
    position,
    promotions,
    plaudits,
    or popularity.

I do not have to be right,
    first,
    tops,
    recognized,
    praised,
    regarded,
    or rewarded.
I now live by faith,
    love by patience,
    live by prayer,
    and labor by power.
My pace is set.
My gait is fast.
My goal is Heaven.
My road is narrow.
My way is rough.
My companions few.
My Guide reliable.
My mission clear.

I cannot be bought,
    compromised,
    deterred,
    lured away,
    turned back,
    diluted,
    or delayed.
I will not flinch in the face of sacrifice.
I will not hesitate in the presence of adversity.
I will not negotiate at the table of the enemy.
I will not ponder at the pool of popularity,
    nor meander in the maze of mediocrity.

I will not give up,
    back up,
    let up,
    or shut up until I have prayed up,
    preached up,
    stored up
    and stayed up the cause of Christ.
I am a disciple of Jesus Christ.

I must go until He returns,
    give until I drop,
    preach until all know,
    and work until He comes.
And when He comes to get His own,
    He will have no trouble recognizing me.
My colors are flying high,
    and they are clear for all to see.
I am a disciple of Jesus Christ.

Are you a disciple of Jesus Christ? It is a free gift to receive by faith alone. But it will cost you everything.

Christian Focus Publications

Our mission statement –

STAYING FAITHFUL

In dependence upon God we seek to impact the world through literature faithful to His infallible Word, the Bible. Our aim is to ensure that the Lord Jesus Christ is presented as the only hope to obtain forgiveness of sin, live a useful life and look forward to heaven with Him.

Our Books are published in four imprints:

CHRISTIAN FOCUS

popular works including biographies, commentaries, basic doctrine and Christian living.

CHRISTIAN HERITAGE

books representing some of the best material from the rich heritage of the church.

MENTOR

books written at a level suitable for Bible College and seminary students, pastors, and other serious readers. The imprint includes commentaries, doctrinal studies, examination of current issues and church history.

CF4•K

children's books for quality Bible teaching and for all age groups: Sunday school curriculum, puzzle and activity books; personal and family devotional titles, biographies and inspirational stories – Because you are never too young to know Jesus!

Christian Focus Publications Ltd,
Geanies House, Fearn, Ross-shire,
IV20 1TW, Scotland, United Kingdom.
www.christianfocus.com